Foreword by
APOSTLE DR. ALFRED KODUAH
Former General Secretary of The Church of Pentecost

The ONLY ONE

EVERY WOMAN'S DREAM

DANIEL & BETTY NYARKO

THE ONLY ONE: *Every Woman's Dream*

CONTENTS

DEDICATION

This book is dedicated to all married couples
everywhere and especially to all husbands who are
committed to making their wives
"The Only Ones" in word and in deed;

To Abigail (who has worked hard to be a living example
of The Only One) and to Grace and Angela
who are faithfully following the trail.

ACKNOWLEDGEMENTS

This work could not have seen the light of day without the immense contributions of various individuals and groups and who we now acknowledge with profound gratitude.

We give all the glory, honour and thanks to the Almighty God who has kept and sustained us through the thick and thin on our marital journey. We are who we are simply by the grace of God! May His Name be praised!

We also want to put on record our heartfelt gratitude to Apostle Dr. Alfred Koduah (former General Secretary of The Church of Pentecost) who graciously accepted to read through the manuscript, made valuable suggestions and wrote the Foreword. Together with your wife, Mama Rachel, you have become our parents both physically and spiritually. May God richly bless you.

Several people encouraged us to put this book together after listening to, and/or participating in some of our counselling sessions. We would like to single out

Madam Stella Dugan for her special words of encouragement. Your words still echo in our ears and we are very grateful.

All the participants and audiences in our various marriage counselling sessions over the years both in Ghana and abroad deserve our appreciation. We have learnt a lot from you too and we ask for God's special blessings upon your lives and marriages. Stay blessed in the Lord!

Our deep appreciation goes to Rev. Godfried and Mrs. Elizabeth Bamfo of the Presbyterian Church of Ghana for your great influence on our lives and for the opportunity given us to be part of Family Impact Ghana. We also wish to acknowledge all the Directors of Family Impact Ghana for the wonderful fellowship we share in impacting families for the sake of the Kingdom of God.

We are deeply indebted to you, Bishop Emmanuel Botwey (General Overseer) and Apostle Dr. Francis Oppong Ankomah (Deputy General Overseer) both of the Christian Faith Church International, for your mentorship and partnering with us in our marriage counselling endeavours.

Thank you so much, Rev. Paul Henry Dsane (Assistant General Superintendent of the Assemblies of

God, Ghana) and your wife, Pastor Mrs. Doris Dsane (both of the Grace Pentecostal Assembly of God, Effiakuma-Takoradi), for your encouragement and personal participation in the several marriage counselling sessions we have had with your Church. You have been a tremendous boost to our efforts in bringing hope and smiles to hurting marriages. To the Couples Fellowship of the Church, we wish to register our most sincere appreciation for your readiness in opening your doors to us. Remain blessed!

It is with gratitude to you, Rev. and Mrs. Newman and to Elder and Mrs. Aryetey, for the invitation extended to us to minister at the wedding of your daughter and son, Charlotte and Charles respectively. The message that has given rise to this book was first given at this wedding and was well received by all. We are happy that Charles still holds Charlotte as his "only one, the perfect one."

To our special family, Tony and Sally Addiabah, Mark and Julie Agyemang, and Joel and Becky Arhin, we say "God bless you" for being a wonderful part of us. Thank you for dutifully and faithfully applying all the principles advocated in this book. You are, indeed, living testimonies that these principles work and will certainly aid other couples to turn things round for good.

Vincent (our son-in-law), Abigail, Grace and Angela (our three Princesses) deserve special mention. You have been wonderful in all things and we pray that God will shower you all with His uncommon blessings and favour every day of your lives.

You cannot be forgotten, Betty, my Queen and my "Only One!" You have been my "jewel of inestimable value" (courtesy of the late Chief Obafemi Awolowo of Nigeria). You wrote parts of this book, recalled most of our shared experiences, proof-read the manuscript several times and offered very useful, practical suggestions. You have been a true embodiment of "The Only One." May God continue to bless you beyond your wildest dreams!

Rev. Prof. Daniel & Mrs. Betty Nyarko
Takoradi, Ghana

FOREWORD

Being God's first institution on earth, marriage is honoured in all cultures. The celebration of marriage in every culture usually goes with some ceremonies and funfair. Those ceremonies and funfair make marriage appear very attractive and enjoyable. Indeed, marriage is attractive and enjoyable, but the hard reality is that it is also a very difficult contractual relationship. The reason is that trying to blend the character and aspirations of a man and a woman together from different backgrounds cannot be taken for granted. Whereas it takes some couples many years to blend their character and aspirations, others are never able to fully achieve any meaningful results. Those who succeed enjoy their marital life as a miniature heaven on earth, but the unsuccessful ones simply endure all the associated disagreements, quarrels and disappointments.

It is for this reason that Rev. Professor Daniel Nyarko and his wife, Betty, have written this insightful book *The Only One: Every Woman's Dream.* The book aims at assisting the unmarried and those preparing for marriages to enable them understand and appreciate what marriage is all about. The book also provides guidelines for saving marriages that are experiencing difficulties.

Right from the very first chapter, Rev. Professor Nyarko and his wife, Betty, strongly recommend that as far as knowing the beauty and ugly sides as well as the ups and downs of marriage are concerned, it is appropriate for marriage couples to consult King Solomon who was able to live with seven hundred wives and three hundred concubines (1 Kgs. 11:3). Simply put, King Solomon was an expert in marital relationships.

Solomon's skills in marital issues are seen in his book Song of Songs, which is as a collection of love poems between a man and a woman. Some tradition has it that the lady in that book was a country girl referred to as Shulammite who had been chastely brought up in the country side by her step-brothers. Her step-brothers had subjected her to so much hard work in the vineyard to the extent that her skin had become dark (SS. 1:5-6). Because of that she felt too inferior to marry. However, when King Solomon met her, he skilfully and lovingly rebuilt her image and married her. The romantic discussions they had are contained in the book. Reading the book with a carnal mind will readily reveal how sensual it is, but one needs go beyond that. There are a lot of spiritual lessons to be learnt. The king in the book depicts King Jesus, who has met a poor woman (the sinner), loved her, washed her and married her. Yes, the King of kings loved wretched sinners, washed and saved them for good works (Rom. 5:8). What a splendid marital picture it is! The Lord has been lovingly taking care of His bride, and preparing her for higher glory. The discourse in the book should be seen in the light of Christ and His bride. Due to the romantic nature of the contents of the book, some tradition has it that conservative Rabbis forbade Jews from reading it until they attained the age of thirty. From the story narrated in the book of Song of Songs, it would be seen that King Solomon made that woman his very special one. Although the woman found herself in a polygamous marriage, she still felt that she was *The Only One*.

Rev. Professor Nyarko and his wife, Betty, have outlined fifteen characteristics of those who qualify for the status of *The Only One* or the 'perfect woman' as being God-fearing, confident, adaptable, trustworthy, industrious, attractive, humble, loyal, emotionally mature, independent, hospitable, affectionate, supportive, honest and generous.

Instead of demonstrating these qualities in marriage, the writers acknowledge that people who are not enjoying their marriages have been caught up in the "Greener Pasture Syndrome," which "describes a situation where a partner loses sight of his or her marital vows and suddenly sees a third party or an outsider as being better, more attractive, or more desirable than his or her spouse". They rightly attribute this unfortunate syndrome to sheer fantasy, fear, compromise and lust. For them, all these lead to marital infidelity, which must be avoided at all costs.

They, therefore, recommend several principles as a panacea to marital problems. These include making God the centre of the marriage, making your spouse the number one person in your life after God, settling your differences the same day without the intervention of a third person, showing interest in whatever your spouse does, as well as leaving, cleaving and becoming one flesh. Furthermore, the writers used the acronym PROTECT to help build strong marriages. These are praying together, rekindling romance, overlooking wrongs, timeliness, encouraging each other, communicating effectively and togetherness.

Additionally, Rev. Professor and Mrs. Nyarko assert that "You can make the difference" as far as saving your marriage is concerned. They declared, "If you desire or dream to make your marriage work, you can do it. It depends on you, but not on your partner. Be the change agent and it will motivate the other person too to change. You cannot change your spouse. No. The change you desire must begin with you and the ripple effect cannot be lost on your spouse." They postulate that this plan ultimately works even if your partner is initially indifferent. In other words, they have provided a plan on how to save your marriage alone. Accordingly, Rev. Professor and Mrs. Nyarko have outlined what couples should be doing to keep their marriages running smoothly. These include renewing dedication and commitment to the Lord, renewing love and commitment to your spouse, mending holes in the marital relationship, staying focused, making a definite decision to avoid mythical 'greener pastures' in marriage, opening a fresh page in the marital relationship, forgiving and tolerating each other, and seeking appropriate help whenever necessary.

Finally, the writers call on couples to change their attitudes by constantly noting that their marriages can always be made better. This can be done through improved mutual respect, communication, meeting each other's needs, spending quality time together, periodically giving gifts and lovingly appreciating one another, making themselves more appealing and attractive as well as committing themselves to the success of the marriage.

This insightful and well-written book *The Only One: Every Woman's Dream* will certainly benefit all Christians who are either preparing to enter marriage and those who are desirous of improving their marital relationships. More importantly, the book is for those whose marriages are going through turbulent times. I believe that through the pages of this book, many such marriages are going to receive healing and restoration. I, therefore, unreservedly recommend this book to Christians – married and unmarried – who are honestly seeking to build their marriage lives to the glory of the Lord.

Apostle Alfred Koduah (PhD)
Former General Secretary of The Church of Pentecost
Area Head, The Church of Pentecost, Takoradi

PREFACE

Marriage as an institution of God has been with mankind since creation when God Himself presided over the first 'wedding' in the Garden of Eden. One would have expected that since God was involved from the beginning, mankind would have given it the honour it deserves. Unfortunately, this is far from the expected. If there is any institution that has been grossly misunderstood, abused and dishonoured over the years in all cultures of the world, it is marriage.

Generations over the years have failed to recognize that the abuse of marriage and promiscuity led to the destruction of two great cities, Sodom and Gomorrah, by God. The world today by the actions of many governments and the behaviours of the people are edging closer to the two great cities, if already not surpassed them.

But, God created the female as a helper to the male and is expected to be respected and treated with decorum. As the 'crown' of God's creation, God intended the woman to be *"the only one."* She was made beautiful to behold, and together with the man, inherited God's command to "be fruitful and increase in number; fill the earth and subdue it" (Gen. 1:28).

The characteristic joy and excitement of the newly-married is exemplified by Adam's bewilderment on seeing Eve by his side and his apt description of her in Genesis 2:23 that:

> *"This is now bone of my bones and flesh of my flesh; she shall be called 'woman,' for she was taken out of man."*

No wonder, then, that since Adam's time, every properly contracted marriage is ushered in with an uncommon joy and excitement. The bride and the groom are both ecstatic at the prospects of coming together. They look into the future with high hopes and expectations. So are their respective families, friends and loved ones. However, living the dream and sustaining it over time has been a mountain too high for several marriages to scale. Several marriages falter and crumble at the base of the mountain before the fifth anniversary. Those who survive the first five years also face the daunting task of combining work with parenting where, in most cases, the husband is a mere passenger. The wife's attention and devotion are directed from the husband to the children and the couple may no longer spend quality time together. If this development is not checked, the couple begins to drift apart and the likelihood for deep-seated, difficult challenges becomes apparent. They do not come in a dramatic fashion but in subtle ways such as simple annoyances and slight misunderstandings but have the potential to turn into a blazing fireball that will consume the marriage.

Where a couple is able to recognize the danger signs and quickly reconcile or seek counsel, they are able to overcome and get back to their winning ways. But this is not that easy. Unfortunately, most couples fail by over-reacting to the developing challenges or by not taking action at all. Both scenarios are not good for the health of the marriage. As counsellors, we have witnessed many marriages go through this dark alley and are almost doomed by the time either one of the couple or both of them take steps to correct the situation.

In this book, we have tried to share our experiences and to highlight the tell-tale signs of impending danger. We believe that when couples heed the pieces of advice found on the pages of this book, they will not fall into the same unpleasant situations others have fallen into or are struggling to overcome. Indeed, there are principles for marital success as contained in the Holy Scriptures and they are also outlined with the hope that anyone who cares to follow them will reap the abundant joys of marriage. We trust that our practical approach to unraveling the thorny issues of marriage will help you identify with the characters in this book. We emphasize that God intended marriage to be enjoyed and so He provided a blueprint for success. We humbly encourage you not only to read to find them but also to apply them heartily to your situation and you will be blessed thereby.

It is, indeed, every woman's dream to be seen, heard and treated as *the only one* by her husband. When a man accords his wife respect as being "the only one," he receives double honour from the wife and blessings from the Lord God which translates into joy, peace, understanding and general happiness in the home. Do you want to be a happily married man? Sure, you do. We pray that the Lord God will give you the grace to humble yourself enough to see, hear and accord your wife the status of being *"the only one."*

CHAPTER ONE

INTRODUCTION

When it comes to talking about marriage, its beauty and ugly sides, its ups and downs, one man who quickly comes to mind to be able to tell us more and candidly advise us is King Solomon. He was the man who got married to seven hundred wives of royal birth and had three hundred concubines (1 Kgs. 11:3). He really loved women, especially foreign women. Concerning the foreign women, it is said that he *"held fast to them in love"* (1 Kgs. 11:1-2). King Solomon must have had his full share of the vicissitudes of marriage and that must explain his love songs in the Bible referred to as the Song of Solomon. No wonder he could describe one of his brides, among his many queens and concubines, in Song 6:9 as:

> *"My dove, my perfect one, is the only one. The only one of her mother, the favourite of the one who bore her. The daughters saw her and called her blessed. The queens and concubines, and they praised her." (NKJV).*

This quotation is one that every husband should know and should be able to say to his wife. Come to think of it. The woman you have taken as your wife was chosen by you from among several women known to you. You picked her carefully and thoughtfully from among all those women who, in one way or the other, came close to you as classmates, playmates, colleagues, team-mates, neighbours, church members, choristers, friends or casual acquaintances. After choosing her, all others should definitely not count. Some men even had difficulty making the choice from among a bevy of ladies who were potential partners. Nonetheless, you settled on one person, the special one, to whom you pledged your life and love "for better for worse, till death do us part."

It is not far-fetched to say that every woman dreams of becoming "the only one" to be loved and cherished by her husband. No woman ever wants to have a rival and will do everything to protect her husband and marriage. Sadly, though, this innate ambition has sometimes been carried too far with very bizarre consequences including permanent injury and death. The Almighty God in His wisdom gave only one woman, Eve, to Adam. She was "the only one," truly loved and cherished by Adam. Surely, every man has the power to follow Adam's example.

At a recent marriage counselling session, a seventy-five year old retired military officer who had been married for forty years emotionally shared his impressions and ended by saying, "Oh, how I wish I had known these truths in my early thirties, before I married!" He held the hands of his aging wife of seventy-two and pledged to redeem all the years he had made her suffer and to make her "the Queen, the only one" for the rest of their lives. This expression of love for a dear one, even at that advanced age, expectedly drew tears from majority of the younger participants who equally pledged to make their wives, the "perfect one, the only one" for as long as they lived.   This drama motivated the authors to put their thoughts and experiences as counsellors together in this book which is in your hands today. It is our prayer that you will be able to see your marriage turned around for the best as you follow and apply the principles contained herein.

Whereas our primary interest in this book is not to provide a blueprint for married couples (much less for post-marital counselling), we still believe that the application of the truths highlighted in the succeeding pages will help save many marriages from hitting the rocks. In addition, the unmarried, those preparing for marriage and pre-marital counsellors may benefit from the pieces of advice and practical experiences shared within. Thus, if after reading this book it dawns on you to make a decision to regard and treat your spouse as "the special one, the only one" who deserves your trust and true love, we would have achieved our aim. After all, that is how you saw her before you took the singular decision to tie the knot with her. She is, and must remain, "the only one." That is the only way to make your marriage an enjoyable experience. It is a worthy choice to make, and it is a rewarding one. So, come with us on the journey to discover how to make her "the special one, the only one," the queen of your dreams.

CHAPTER TWO

CHARACTERISTICS OF "THE ONLY ONE"

It is a fact of life that every young person dreams of marrying the man or woman who fits his or her description of a "perfect spouse." Male or female, we all tend to have an imaginary "perfect spouse," *the only one,* who meets a certain criteria in mind. But do we always have it the way we wanted or dreamt of? Is it possible to have a "perfect spouse" as King Solomon described for us? Look at the following true story. Only their real names have been changed to protect their identity.

Sam and Philip had been childhood friends and classmates until they both passed their common entrance examinations and parted ways for their secondary school education. Sam attended one of the best schools in the nation's capital city while Philip enrolled in a local secondary school. Sam continued his education at the university. Philip, unfortunately, dropped out of school on the death of his father. Several years had passed and the friends had lost contact with each other. Recently, as fate would have it, the two friends bumped into each other at a shopping mall in the city.

"Hey, Philip, is that you?" Sam called out in astonishment.

"What a surprise!" Philip replied. They shook hands.

"Life has been good to you, I can see." Sam emphasized and almost regretted his admission of the reality of life.

"So, where have you been all these years, Sam?"

"It's a long story, my brother. Let's find a seat so that we can fill each other up."

The two friends entered a nearby restaurant and settled down. They ordered drinks and meals. For almost two hours they talked about their lives. It turned out that when Philip dropped out of school, he did menial jobs to survive. By dint of hard work, he had become a successful businessman with a wife and four kids. Sam, on the other hand, had graduated from the university and secured a lucrative job in the civil service. But he was hesitant in talking about his family life with Philip who, in the spirit of true friendship, invited him home for dinner. Sam gladly accepted the invitation.

Later that evening, Sam arrived at the plush residence of his bosom friend and was unprepared for what he witnessed. The warm reception he received from Philip's wife when he was introduced to her made his eyes blurred with tears. Though married, he had never felt this warmth at home. He braced himself up for the evening and watched with bewilderment the affection and respect between Philip and his wife, Becky. Soon, he was invited to a sumptuous dinner for which he showed great appreciation.

After dinner, the two friends had time to chat before Sam took his leave. "Oh, how I wish my wife had been like yours. You have a wonderful wife and very happy children." Sam finally opened up on his marital life.

"I am sure your wife is equally good, if not better," Philip quipped.

"You have no idea what I have been through. I've lost my job for almost two years now. I am finding it difficult to secure another," bemoaned Sam.

"What happened?"

"It's all because of Rita. I married her for her beauty, but I have learnt my lesson. We had been having challenges at home throughout our thirteen years of marriage. Rita walked into my office one day and picked up a quarrel with me. Some colleagues came in to broker peace including my secretary who was severely assaulted. She was hospitalized for days. That unruly behaviour cost me my job."

"I am sorry about that. I hope things are getting better."

"On the contrary, Rita deserted me about a month ago on account of our financial difficulties. She left our two young children behind."

"Where is Rita now and how are you coping with the kids?"

"My mother-in-law confirmed that Rita has travelled abroad and wants divorce. Since I could not cater for the children, I have sent them to my big sister. I will go for them when the dust settles. I deeply regret the day I set my eyes on Rita."

Sam thanked God for Philip's life and for the opportunity of meeting him again. Philip, as a mark of true friendship, offered to employ Sam as the Group General Manager of his businesses.

The sad experiences of Sam may sound familiar in

several aspects. Every couple begins the marital journey on a good, happy note. Indeed, every couple on their wedding day ties the knot with great expectations of a happy, fulfilled marital life. Sam, with his academic credentials thought that marrying beautiful Rita was all that mattered. Beauty is important but character is essential. A woman without character is like a clinging cymbal whose sound fades away with time. One would hesitate to compare Rita to Philip's wife. But Sam saw something in Becky he had never seen in Rita: her simplicity, the warmth in her smiles and respect for her husband! Someone had said that:

> *"Most people get married believing a myth that marriage is a beautiful box full of all the things they have longed for: companionship, intimacy, friendship, etc. The truth is that marriage at the start is an empty box. You must put something in before you can take anything out. There is no love in marriage. Love is in people. And people put love in marriage. There is no romance in marriage. You have to infuse it into your marriage. A couple must learn the art and form the habit of giving, loving, serving, praising, keeping the box full. If you take out more than you put in, the box will be empty."* [Anonymous]

Who, then, is the "perfect spouse"? What distinguishes this spouse from all others? In other words, what are the characteristics of the "perfect one"? To find the right answers to these questions and similar ones, it is expedient to begin with the Bible. And what better picture do we have than Proverbs 31 which describes the "perfect woman" from a godly woman's perspective. In Proverbs 31, King Lemuel (who is believed by many Bible scholars to be the same King Solomon) writes a comprehensive description of the *virtuous, ideal, excellent* or *perfect* woman whom he also calls *"the perfect one," "the only one"* later in Song 6:9. Those were the words of wisdom from a mother to his son (King Lemuel) on finding a good wife, an excellent wife. It is sad that men, like Sam, very often seek a wife for very transient reasons: beauty, height, style, education, money, accomplishment. All these, and many more external wrappings, are wrong reasons. Rather, emphasis should be on a woman's inner beauty which is exemplified by her virtues, strength of character and spiritual excellence.

On the basis of the advice of the mother of King Lemuel, we find that the "perfect one" is a woman who is God-fearing, humble, trustworthy, ingenious, inherently good, kind, wise, prudent, thrifty, respectful, industrious, confident, dependable, clever, generous, joyful, dutiful and watchful, among others. These are qualities that make any woman, (such as Becky in the opening story), beautiful inside out. These qualities characterize what is good, desirable and lasting in a woman. After all, we know that outward beauty is fleeting and charm is deceptive, but a woman who fears God is to be praised! (Pro. 31:30)

In our world today, the concept of the "excellent woman" has attracted attention from a multitude of well-meaning people. These include Bible scholars, marriage counsellors, psychologists, sociologists, historians and social commentators, just to mention a few. Their definitions and characteristics of the ideal woman are as varied as the amount of literature available. This is because "beauty lies in the eyes of the beholder." Simply, what is "beautiful" in the eyes of one man or scholar may be significantly different from the point of view of another scholar. It is, therefore, not common to have a unanimously agreed list of characteristics or qualities that marks out the "perfect one." Every individual does have his or her list of what makes up the characteristics of the ideal spouse. In the light of the foregoing, we will like to present the following carefully-selected fifteen qualities as the components of the desirable characteristics of the "perfect one." Becky, with due respect, can be said to possess a large measure of these qualities, if not all. The "perfect one" is the woman who is:

i. God-fearing: Above all else, we believe that a woman who fears God possesses the ultimate quality. The Bible says in Proverbs 31:30 that such a woman is to be praised (commended or celebrated). In Strong's Dictionary of Hebrew and Greek words, the expression "she shall be praised" also means *"she shall be given in marriage."* Thus, in searching for a wife, the best, over-riding quality to look out for is to find one who fears the Lord. Similarly, it can be said that young men who will make the best husbands are those who are God-fearing. Do you or your spouse possess this quality?

ii. Confident: A confident person is one who is very much sure of whatever he or she is doing. That person is well-educated, intelligent and on top of issues. The perfect one, therefore, shows confidence in her speech, attitudes, and in the discharge of her marital duties such as cooking, washing, general house-keeping, reception of guests, and meeting the emotional needs of her husband. She is bold but not saucy. Whether she has had formal or informal education, her level of confidence and intelligence cannot be questioned.

iii. Adaptable: The ability to adapt to situations at very short notice is a quality that marks out the ideal woman. Conditions and circumstances may not always be as one would like or as one planned it. However, rising to the occasion at any given moment calls for flexibility, creativity or adaptability. Sarah (Abraham's wife) showed this quality when she was requested at short notice to prepare a meal for the three guests her husband invited home (Gen. 18:1-8). She neither complained nor gave excuses. She passed the test and received the promise of a son. How adaptable are you? Do you always meet changing situations with complaints and grumblings? Health and wealth, for example, may not always be as one would want them to be. So, learn to be creative and adaptable.

iv. Trustworthy: The "perfect one" is a woman who can be trusted to the hilt. The Bible says of such a woman that *"the heart of her husband safely trusts her"* (Pro. 31:11, NKJV). Even in ordinary or casual friendships, trust is a key quality required of the friends to keep them together. Of course, two persons cannot *"walk together unless they have agreed to do so"* (Amos 3:3). Trust is an important quality that must be present in any relationship to ensure success. If a husband cannot trust his wife, and vice versa, the marriage is destined for the rocks. Let us do everything to develop trust and to become trustworthy in all spheres of life.

v. Industrious: If there is one visible quality every man wants to find in a wife, it is her being industrious. No one wants a lazy woman as a spouse. The ideal woman does not lack in industry. She is busy from morning till nightfall. She ensures that her home is neat and attractive. Food (and good quality meals as such) are not lacking in the home at any point in time. She takes very good care of her husband as well as the children in a fashionable way. A casual visitor to the home can easily tell when she is absent. Any time she is away, she is dearly missed by the husband and the family as a whole. Are you missed whenever you are away?

vi. Attractive: The "perfect one" knows how to keep herself attractive for her husband and be presentable always. She takes good care of her body and maintains her dignity through her dressing and appearance. She endeavours to remain romantic. She keeps her hair neat and smells nice irrespective of her hard work. She does the same for her husband and ensures that he always has neat, ironed and fresh clothes to wear. Childbirth and ageing do not diminish her attractiveness. They rather enhance the fine lines and contours of her body such that her husband is perpetually attracted to her. She is neither ahead nor far behind current fashion trends. As an ideal woman, how do you measure in attractiveness? Do you no longer pay attention to your appearance? Be careful not to overlook your physical appearance or attractiveness.

vii. Humble: Humility is a well-known quality but one that is very difficult for some people to possess. In a marital relationship, both partners should exhibit this quality towards each other for peace, understanding and success to be attained. The humility of a wife to her husband is enjoined by the Scriptures. It shows in the wife's submission to her own husband (Eph. 5:22). Biblical submission is not servitude and does not amount to the loss of the wife's human rights. It means that the wife willingly subjects her own will and wishes to that of her husband who is the head of the family. After all, there cannot be two captains in one ship! Where humility is reciprocal between husband and wife as admonished in Ephesians 5:21, the relationship prospers and the partners grow in love and affection towards each other. The ideal or perfect woman is not swayed by the world's interpretation of "submission" knowing fully well that submission to her own husband is submission to the Lord.

viii. Loyal: The loyalty and commitment of the "perfect one" to her husband is as clear as crystal. Her faith in her husband to take care of the family and to do the right thing at all times propels her to give her best. She remains resolutely committed to the success of the marriage and will always work towards that end. She understands that marriage is a life-long relationship that is not to be broken at will until death. Thus, her preoccupation is to live or die for the success of the marital bond. No storm of life can shake her faith in her husband. Certainly, no changes in her expectations, no matter how negative, can cause her to look back. She does not do things behind her husband or on his blind side. She is transparent, honest, in all her dealings. How committed are you to the success of your marriage? How loyal are you to your husband? Are you keeping secrets unknown to him? Do well to stay loyal and committed to your own marital relationship.

ix. Emotionally Mature: Many people who enter into marriages are physically matured but emotionally immature. They find it difficult to contain the changing scenes of life and, least of all, the shortcomings in their spouses. An emotionally matured woman is the one who is able to laugh and smile even in difficult times. The "perfect one" ably controls circumstances within her power and does not throw tantrums, nag or weep unnecessarily. She is a good listener but speaks few words. She abhors gossip and keeps her marital issues private. She always speaks well of her husband in all circumstances and at all places. She is wise to build her home and does not tear it down with her own hands (Pro. 14:1). She is always ready to act positively but does not easily react to challenges without a prior analysis of the situation. Are you the type who easily reacts to challenges without taking time to think through? Are you given to nagging and shedding of tears at the least provocation? If it is so, then you must prayerfully work on your emotional maturity without further delay. You may need to seek help from a seasoned marriage counsellor or psychologist.

x. Independent: The "perfect one" asserts her independence. She does not cling to her husband like a leech. She does not depend on her husband for every little thing in life. She has a career or is professionally engaged in a trade. She has a vision and follows it. She does not throw her vision overboard on account of marriage. She keeps her own world of friends and has something she is passionate about outside the home. For example, she gets involved in Church activities and serves as a children's teacher, Sunday school teacher, chorister, prayer warrior and the like. Are you *completely dependent* on your spouse? Find something to do and show that you have what it takes to be on your own. Where an "ideal woman" is not gainfully employed, it must be by mutual consent of her spouse.

xi. Hospitable: Another well-known quality of the "perfect one" is her hospitality. She welcomes everyone to her home and takes care of them, strangers and family members alike. There is always food and water for everyone who passes by or makes a stop-over at her home.

She is a brilliant chef who knows what is good for the family in terms of providing them with the right diet. She wears a warm smile every time and all are made to feel at home, even away from home. Her presence brings warmth to the weary soul and her family never grows hungry. She takes a keen interest in what her husband eats, drinks and wears. She always goes the extra mile to make others happy.

xii. Affectionate: The "perfect one" knows how to show affection to the one whom she loves. Of course, she shows affection to all, but she reserves a special one for her spouse. She is appreciative of the little things done for her by her husband and by people around her. She endeavours to keep the flame of romance burning brightly. She never gets tired of expressing her love and appreciation to her husband at every opportunity. She is ready to hug or be hugged, hold hands, kiss and touch lovingly. She has nice things to say about her spouse and she never runs him down. Among her peers, she always presents her husband as the king. How do you see your own husband or wife? How do you treat him or her? Do you treat him or her with so much love and affection or with hatred and disdain?

xiii. Supportive: To say that the "perfect woman" is supportive of her husband might be an understatement.

She is the embodiment of support, total in its ramifications. She is an excellent pillar that grounds the family and propels her spouse to greater heights. Her words are filled with encouragement for the husband and children at all times. Even when the going gets tough, she can be relied upon to make the journey look shorter and the burden much lighter. Her words build up and lift flagging spirits. She motivates and inspires others to achieve the utmost. Are you supportive of your spouse or you are a doomsday prophetess? The words we speak have power. Use them wisely.

xiv. Honest: Honesty has always been a cherished quality. Everyone loves an honest person but it is not everyone who is honest. The "perfect one" is an honest woman who will always deal truthfully with her husband and every other person for that matter. She is sought after. Make her the treasurer of the Church or social group and you are sure the finances will be kept safe and in order. She brings the same quality to managing her home. She speaks the truth always in love as the Bible admonishes (Eph. 4:15). What is the level of your honesty? Do you choose to be honest when it suits the occasion but turns the other way when being honest will hurt? The Scriptures admonish that *"whoever walks in integrity walks securely, but whoever takes crooked paths will be found out"* and that *"the integrity of the upright guides* *them, but the unfaithful are destroyed by their duplicity"* (Pro. 10:9 and Pro. 11:3 respectively). It pays to be honest.

xv. Generous: The "perfect one," no doubt, is a generous woman. She is a giver, always ready to share whatever she has with others. At Church or in the neighbourhood, she is known for her generosity. Her family and the family of her spouse testify of her spirit of giving. She shows uncommon concern for meeting the needs of others and draws her husband's attention to such needs. Her kindness is not only by giving away material things, she has kind words for all. She goes the extra mile to ensure that her husband is happy all the time. She makes it a habit to surprise her spouse with gifts, not only on special occasions like birthdays and wedding anniversaries, but also on ordinary days, out of turn. Such little acts of generosity oil the wheels of romantic love and keep the marriage flourishing and blossoming, and being evergreen on all days.

Conclusion: Being a special couple, the envy of your peers and all observers, is not far-fetched. It depends on what you decide to make of your spouse. Your happiness depends on the happiness of your spouse. In other words, if you want to be happy in your marriage, seek the happiness of your spouse. Do the little things you used to do for him or her before you tied the knot. Help your spouse to give her best and you will enjoy the relationship. You can turn your spouse into the "special one, the only one" of your dreams when you encourage her to break out of her cocoon and shine. Every woman has what it takes to be the "special one." It is the circumstances and the situations they face after they have given their consent by saying, "Yes, I do," that turns them into "something else." As a husband, you do not need to look far. The "special one, the only one" is just by your side waiting to be discovered!

CHAPTER THREE

THE "GREENER PASTURE SYNDROME"

Many years ago at a teacher training college in Ghana, a debate on the merits and demerits of marrying at a younger age was successfully held by the Debating Club. After the interesting academic-cum-moral exercise, a group of senior students gathered in front of one of the halls of residence and engaged in a heated yet lively debate of their own. The enthusiasm with which they discussed the issues attracted a fairly large crowd of other students. Senior Moses, the respected and fairly elderly man who was the dining hall prefect, set the tone of the discussions when he stated categorically that:

"It is a good thing to marry while young, when you are still strong and working. I am happy to be married with five children now."

Andy, the sports prefect, quickly cut in: "Oh ho, holy Moses! Five kids now? No wonder you look old and worn out. Are all the kids from the same woman?"

Moses: "Yes. I have only one wife. I have been married to Monica for the past fifteen years."

Mark: "Have you had any girlfriends besides her?"

Moses: "No. I am satisfied with her."

Andy: "You've done well. But I can't stay with one woman for that long. I will be bored to death. Right now, I have three girlfriends."

Moses: "Why not? Why can't you stay with only one girl and be loyal to her?"

Andy: "It is not a good idea to eat the same meal over and over again. You need a variety to have a balanced diet."

The crowd that had gathered and had been listening burst into laughter. Several other speakers supported Andy's viewpoint. Mike came in strongly saying that he too cannot stay with one woman since having several partners makes one feel manly. Jimmy said that he had been married for barely two years and had already been seeing another woman. His reason was that he liked slim women but since his wife delivered about ten months ago, she has grown so fat that he is no longer attracted to her. That explains why he was seeing slender Bridget, a final year undergraduate student, and already contemplating divorcing his wife to marry Bridget when she completed her studies. After all, he had been sponsoring her education.

Moses: "Andy, your problem is that you are comparing a woman to food in your quest for variety. I told you I am satisfied with Monica and I don't need anyone other than her. Besides, she gives me the variety you talk about so our sexual life is not boring the way you think."

"Wow! That's interesting. I wish I can have a wife like Monica," Mark said admiringly and the little crowd applauded.

Joe, the college chaplain, who had joined the group a few moments earlier, offered a piece of advice saying, "Gentlemen, multiple partners can give you short-lived pleasure but can leave you with a big time disease. Stay with one partner and avoid misery tomorrow."

Charlie, the college jester, added: "Everyone thinks I am a fool. But one thing I don't go near is having multiple partners. I love my wife and I don't want to catch any disease that I may inadvertently transfer to her."

"Excellent, Charlie, you have made my day; I need to

catch some sleep," Moses said amidst applause and with that the students started dispersing to their various halls of residence.

It is clear from the episode narrated above that happy, fulfilling marriages do not just happen. The couple must have the right mental attitudes and recognize the fact that marriage is God's creation (Gen. 2:18). Marriage is on the heart of God. This means that to have a beautiful, joyous and lasting marriage, the relationship should be built on sound biblical principles (which are dealt with in the next chapter). These are God-given principles because God Himself is interested in your marriage. He is the witness in your marriage (Mal. 2:14) and He rejoices when couples are happy (Isa. 62:5).

God intended marriages to be enjoyed and not to be endured. When a couple, therefore, enjoys their marriage they become secured and entertain no fear because perfect love casts out fear (1 Jn. 4:18). When the children see their parents happily enjoying their marriage, it affects them positively and they too are happy and feel secured. They have no cause to fear the future. As the parents make God the centre of their marriage, the children learn from them and carry it into their own marriages later in life. Similarly, neighbours, relatives and friends also enjoy the Christ-centred marriage since the peace and joy that radiate from that marriage also affect them in a positive way. Such a happy, fulfilling marriage becomes the toast of all and a model for both the married and unmarried to follow.

If it is true that God instituted marriage and is interested in the marriage covenant as a witness, then why do many marriages fail? There are several reasons but the biggest and most common is what has come to be known among marriage counsellors and psychologists as the "greener pasture syndrome." This has come from the common cliché that "the grass is always green on the other side." But this is an illusion and nothing is far from the truth than this.

What is the "Greener Pasture Syndrome"?

The "greener pasture syndrome" describes a situation where a partner loses sight of his or her marital vows and suddenly sees a third party, an outsider, as being better, more attractive, or more desirable than his or her spouse. A feeling of "Oh, I made a mistake," suddenly begins to take over the mind and his or her critical thought process. This is more common among men than with women. The book of Proverbs 9:17-18 warns that:

> *"Stolen water is sweet; food eaten in secret is delicious! But little do they know that the dead are there, that her guests are deep in the realm of the dead."*

Again, we read in Proverbs 20:17 that:

"Food gained by fraud tastes sweet, but one ends up with a mouth full of gravel."

The partner who has been stung by the "greener pasture syndrome" suddenly begins to see the "imperfections" in his or her spouse (which were overlooked when they first met) and starts to look elsewhere for affection and satisfaction. All too soon, the partner suffering the syndrome gets to think and rationalize that he or she was wrong in choosing the spouse. Invariably, he or she begins to compare the spouse with other couples or persons. The partner who is experiencing this syndrome is evidently going through a significant struggle with his or her level of commitment to the success of the marriage. That partner will need help to overcome but, habitually, such persons find it difficult to admit that they have a problem and that they require assistance to restore things to normalcy. Where the partner admits the problem, the couple can work to resolve things without the intervention of a counsellor or therapist. Unfortunately, most people fail to admit their challenges.

Causes of the "Greener Pasture Syndrome"

What are the common causes of the "greener pasture syndrome"? There is always a reason for a behavioural change in an individual. Four most common causes of the "greener pasture syndrome," according to seasoned psychologists and marriage counsellors, are fantasy, fear, compromise and sheer lust. Let us look at each of these causes in some detail.

i. Fantasy

When a partner drifts into the world of fantasy, it makes him or her believe that "the grass is always greener on the other side" and that "there is something better out there I am missing." Such a partner is sucked up. With that fantasy, he or she is prepared to sacrifice the safety, stability, security and satisfaction of his or her present situation for a "feeling" that there is something better elsewhere. That is when such persons begin to see the other woman (or man) as being better than their spouses in terms of beauty, wealth, education, social standing or any other fleeting yardstick. They get so carried away by their fantasies that they fail to reason. They tend to throw reason and rational behaviour away as they persist in their world of fantasy. No amount of promptings from close family and friends on the dangers ahead is ever heeded to.

But, come to think of it: all that glitters is not gold! Many have gone this way and woefully regretted later. Very few that descend into the "Disney world" of fantasy and fairy tales (where every conceivable desire is attainable) ever get back on track as fully restored. They end up with strained and hurting relationships. They miss the point of reconciliation and painfully lose out on a once thriving relationship.

Watch out if you are beginning to tread the path of fantasy! You might be on a free-fall flight into a world of misery and regret. That is a sure trajectory of failure and many who have gone this way wake up to a life of painful memories that offer no hope of turning around for good. Beware!

ii. Fear

Fear is another common cause of the "greener pasture syndrome." Fear is a feeling that something bad, dangerous, painful or harmful is about to happen. It is a potent force that compels people to act in an often bizarre manner. In the case of marital relationships, the fear of boredom, failure, rejection, oppression, peer pressure and loss of one's individuality are compelling forces that push partners to act in very much unacceptable ways.

When a partner begins to fear that he or she has failed to live up to expectation as a husband or wife, the tendency is for that partner to find solace in persons and things outside the marriage. For example, where a couple faces delayed pregnancy, the probability of the partners fearing for the worse is very high. While the wife may fear she is barren, the husband may at the same time fear that he is infertile or simply impotent. Without prayer, counselling and medical intervention, each of the partners may want to prove that the problem is with the other party. Each party asserts his or her innocence. The danger is that marital infidelity may creep into the relationship with its often destructive consequences. Remember that *"there is no fear in love. But perfect love drives out fear, because fear has to do with punishment. The one who fears is not made perfect in love"* (1 Jn. 4:18).

iii. Compromise

Compromise is when one finds it expedient to accept a standard that is lower than desirable. Compromise in itself is not always a bad idea. There can be a positive compromise which reduces friction between parties and allows a meeting of minds and reconciliation. That happens when the parties in conflict make concessions on each side, a sort of shifting the goal post, in order to achieve an agreement. On the other hand, negative compromise tends to reduce a person's self-worth and permits mediocrity instead of maintaining high standards. Usually, in the marital circles, partners who fear or frown on commitment are quick to compromise on their values, needs and desires. They believe that they can get whatever they want on their own terms elsewhere.

A partner who lacks commitment to the marriage union is ready to do anything without regard for the feelings and ideals of the other partner. Such partners tend to be very selfish since they seek their own interests and not the collective good of the union. They only consider their own immediate satisfaction rather than the long-term good of the relationship. So, it is easier for such a partner to make compromises. The usual self-defensive statements for indulging in unhealthy compromises include: "Oh, it doesn't matter," "it doesn't spoil anything," "this won't hurt a fly," "everybody is doing it," and "he or she won't notice it." Watch out for these statements. They are precursors of something ominous that is about to happen or already happening.

iv. Lust

Sheer lust, pure and simple, is another worrying cause of the "greener pasture syndrome." Some people are never satisfied with what they have and will always be craving for something more. Sometimes, something that is outside their reach. There are men who are fascinated by anyone in skirt and blouse. Worse still, in these days, there are a large number of women, young and old, who take delight in advertising their natural endowments such as their breasts, thighs and legs. There are also men who are ready customers and would jump at every offer. The Hollywood culture of "anything goes" is fast taking over the world and killing the hitherto cherished cultures of the innocent world.

Remember the conversation among the group of teachers-in-training at the beginning of this chapter? A man like Andy who thinks that changing women is like creating a variety in food preferences, will find it easier to indulge in extra-marital affairs. After all, by his mentality or philosophy, he sees nothing wrong at all in lusting after other women. Andy justifies his lust with his eagerness to kill boredom. But, it takes a couple to create an atmosphere of joy and happiness where there is no room for boredom.

Just as some men will do everything to satisfy their insatiable lust, so do some women do things considered taboos a few years back. There are countless cases of men, masters of their homes, taking undue advantage of their step-daughters and house-helps in order to satisfy their lust. Sometime last year, the newspapers were awash with the scandalous news of a respected public servant who put his personal secretary in the family way. Unable to stand the shame and the public disgrace, he took his own life. Instances also abound of married women sleeping with their drivers, gardeners and other men on the blind side of their husbands. Recently, a lady admitted on a radio phone-in programme in Accra that she had been cheating on her husband with the husband's best friend who was the "best man" at their wedding. The husband has no idea of this and is still best of friends with his diabolical buddy.

Conclusion

Marital infidelity these days is becoming like child's play. A lot of people do not seem to subscribe to the age-long core family values of faithfulness to their spouses and commitment to their marital vows. The concept of variety seems to hold a magic wand for many, but they always pay dearly for such acts of indiscretion. Instead of thinking that the grass is greener on the other side, partners should team up and work on their own grass to make it as green as they want it to be. This will require a lot of hard work and the goodwill to make things work for the couple. You have what it takes to make your spouse look like the other woman, and better. The way forward is what is covered in the next chapter.

CHAPTER FOUR

PROTECTING YOUR MARRIAGE

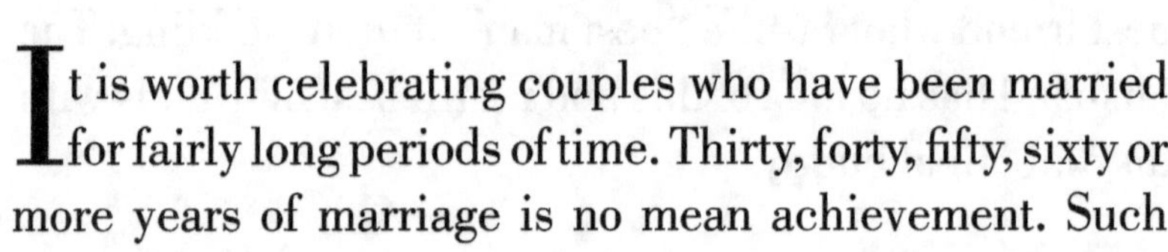

It is worth celebrating couples who have been married for fairly long periods of time. Thirty, forty, fifty, sixty or more years of marriage is no mean achievement. Such couples deserve the award of special medals. Unfortunately, there are no "long service" awards for such committed couples.

Mr. and Mrs. Peterson recently celebrated their forty-fifth marriage anniversary which was organized by their children. It was a grand occasion with several high society and well-meaning personalities in attendance. The tall list of invited guests also included renowned men of God and celebrities who joyously wished the Petersons well and showered them with gifts. A day after the ceremony, Mrs. Peterson received a phone call from a lady who identified herself as Nancy, a friend of Tricia who is Mrs. Peterson's eldest daughter. Nancy sounded as someone who was deeply troubled and requested to seek advice from Mrs. Peterson. She willingly consented and invited Nancy home.

In less than an hour Nancy drove in and was warmly welcomed by Mrs. Peterson. With teary eyes, Nancy told her story of abuse and unhappiness in her six years of marriage and confessed that she had been considering divorce for a while now until she heard the testimony of Mrs. Peterson at the ceremony the previous day. On the advice of Tricia, she decided to meet her for counselling on what to do to enjoy her marriage.

"My dear, I thank God for your life and for making it here today," Mrs. Peterson began.

"Notwithstanding your frustrations and unhappiness, I want you to believe that all is not lost. It shall be well."

With tears streaming down her cheeks, Nancy cut in, "But how can this be when everything I do is not appreciated by my husband?"

"Don't you worry, Sweetheart, there are principles to help you succeed in your marriage," Mrs. Peterson assured Nancy. "These principles have helped us in our marriage and have brought us this far."

Nancy who now looked more sober sat up well and asked, "But Mummy, if there are principles to guide marriages, why are we not taught early? What are these principles?"

"There is no school where the art and science of marriage are taught. Marriage is the only institution where you receive your certificate before you begin," Mrs. Peterson answered and added, "But God who first instituted marriage has given us principles to follow to achieve success and happiness."

Nancy wryly said, "I am ready to learn and apply these principles, but Ben is the problem."

"No. Your husband is not the issue here," Mrs. Peterson explained. "He is not here. You are here. You see, you cannot change Ben. No amount of your nagging or complaining will ever change Ben. That is the mistake most spouses make. You, yourself, have to change in order to change him. When he sees changes in your attitude towards him and other family issues, it will challenge him to make amends."

"I have never known or considered that, Nancy confessed. "I have always thought that the problem is Ben himself and that if only he can change, our marriage will also change for the better. I still love him, you know."

"Let me give you a few more tips before I talk about the principles," Mrs. Peterson said while adjusting her posture in the chair and using her fingers as counters.

"First and foremost, endeavour to make God the centre of your marriage. When you leave Him out, you are doomed. Be more prayerful and keep on praying for Ben. Secondly, your husband should be the number one person in your life after God. Not the children. Adore him and let him feel he is the King."

"Mummy, I have been doing that. It is just that Ben refuses to see or appreciate whatever I do for him," Nancy bemoaned her situation.

"We will get to that pretty soon. But let me finish the tit-bits. Number three is that the two of you should settle your differences the same day and without the intervention of a third person. Don't push today's misunderstandings to tomorrow. Make sure you will be the first to apologize and say, "Honey, I am sorry," even when you are the offended party. That way, you win him back. Marital disagreements are not competitive fields where there should be winners and losers. Couples should always seek win-win results in their conflicts and the best medicine to secure this is in the three words, "I am sorry," from a genuine heart. How difficult, unfortunately, it is for couples to say "I am sorry" to each other!"

Nancy made an attempt to say something but Mrs. Peterson waved her down and continued her pieces of advice.

"The fourth point is that you should show interest in whatever he does so that you can get closer to each other. Try to do things together such as praying, reading the Bible, visiting friends and family, eating, watching the television news and taking care of the children. Fifthly, never compare him to any other person no matter the odds. Finally, always speak words of encouragement to him; never scold or abuse him because he is your husband, not your child. He is your King."

Mrs. Peterson looked up at the clock on the wall and smiled while parting Nancy on the shoulder: "My dear, so soon it is almost two hours since you arrived. I think it is getting late and will not be prudent to continue. I am glad you have calmed down very well and I hope that we can continue our discussions tomorrow or at any time you are free to pay me a visit again."

Nancy could not find words fitting enough to thank Mrs. Peterson for the time she had spent with her and for the 'precious gems' she had received from her. She also assured the elderly woman that she was ready to start the change agenda from herself and would return for the talk on the principles of marriage. With that show of gratitude, she took her leave with the determination and confidence that she will succeed in turning things around in her marriage.

Biblical Principles

We know that marriage is God's own creation. He made the woman purposely for the man, according to the Scriptures, to be his helper and companion. Out of this union, God gives children as gifts. God being the originator did not leave His creation clueless as to what to do to succeed in life as married persons. He has given us a blueprint for success in our marital lives. The blueprint consists of fool-proof principles that assure success for everyone who diligently applies them.

"Let us begin by re-emphasizing some basic truths," Mrs. Peterson informed Nancy on the second day of her visit. "It is very important to recognize that:

i). "Happy fulfilling marriages do not happen by chance. Both partners have the responsibility to work on their marriage to make it successful. Even where the partners believe that their marriage was/is "made in heaven," they must wake up to the reality that the marriage will have to be lived on earth where the environment and other factors, controllable and uncontrollable, may buffet them. The couple will have to continue to regard each other as "the perfect one," the same "perfect" person from the beginning of the relationship. Times and circumstances may change. But the spouse you took can remain the same or be better as life chisels and smoothens the rough edges in each other's character.

ii). "Successful marriages are built on sound biblical principles which puts God at the centre of everything. This is because God instituted marriage and it is on His heart (Gen. 2:18) since that is the way He blessed mankind to share in the mystery of creation.

iii). "In addition, the Lord is especially interested in your marriage because He is the witness of the covenant between you and the wife of your youth (Mal. 2:14). This is very important: your marriage to your "first" and "only" wife (and let her be truly the only wife), the only one. God is ready to help you out on your marital journey to success. Generally, God expects your current wife to be the "only" one.

iv). "It is interesting to know that God is happy and rejoices when couples are happy (Isa. 62:5). This is a fool-proof assurance that you can daily depend on God for good success.

v). "Marriage is a life-long covenant relationship with no room given for abrogation (1 Cor. 7:39). In other words, it is expected to last "till death" without any excuse for divorce (Mal. 2:16). That is the reason for God's emphatic declaration that He "hates divorce." "

Mrs. Peterson continued: "When God instituted marriage in the Garden of Eden, He also gave the principles by which couples will succeed and be happy. It is important to note that there was no father and no mother at the time God established the principles. Yet, God talked about parents when laying out the principles. He laid bare these principles in Genesis 2:24." Nancy was called to read the verse as follows:

"Therefore shall a man leave his father and his mother, and shall cleave unto his wife: and they shall be one flesh." (KJV)

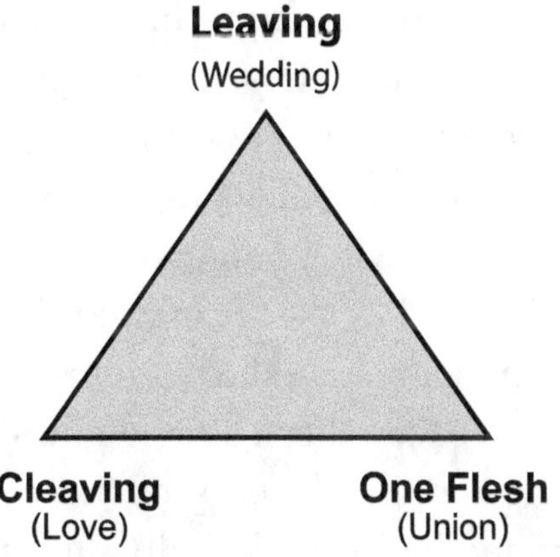

"From the passage, we see clear principles for happy and successful marriages," Mrs. Peterson continued. She went on to list the principles as: leaving, cleaving and becoming one flesh. This is such a fundamental biblical truth that Jesus Christ referred to it in Matthew 19:5 and Mark 10:7 while Apostle Paul also mentioned it in Ephesians 5:31. These three principles constitute "pillars" which form the "marriage triangle."

"All the three pillars of the tripod must be present in order to give a solid support to the marriage. The absence of any one of them means that the foundation of the marriage is shaky and may not survive and grow. One can enter into marriage through any of the three angles of the triangle but the best entrance is through the 'leaving' angle," Mrs. Peterson summarized.

1. The Principle of Leaving: This is the first biblical principle every couple must observe if they are to become happy and successful. It is the desire of every man to leave home at some point in time to seek a life partner and to cleave to her. Leaving father and mother is both *physical* (as evidenced by the social wedding ceremony) and *psychological* (as seen in the readiness of the couple to be committed to each other). Leaving implies the total severance of the umbilical cords of the couple to the comfort and protection of their individual parents and homes (Gen. 24:57-60). The young couple must learn to break free from the direct influence of both parents as well as siblings to start their own new home. Where this physical condition is not satisfied and the young couple makes their marital home in the family home of either the husband's or wife's parents, the marriage is bound to face challenges. The independence of the young couple is compromised and parental control and influence cannot be wished away. It must be emphasized that without proper *leaving*, there can be no proper *cleaving*!

Quite often, in the African setting, we see the woman always *leaving* her home to join her husband in the man's family home. This should not be the rule but an exception, for a short period of time only, just to enable the new couple settle down and find their own accommodation. Every new couple, as well as old couples who are still struggling with this principle, is encouraged to make leaving a priority. However, it must be emphasized that leaving does not imply abandonment. The couple must not neglect their responsibilities of love and care for the parents they leave behind as they establish their new home.

It is equally important that the young wife learns to sever the "umbilical cord" that ties her to her mother. In other words, she should not be running to her mother at the least opportunity with issues from her marriage, whether big or small. The young wife's willingness to leave home and to be with her husband implies that she is ready to play her roles as a wife and a mother to her own children. That should motivate her to keep the young family's marital issues strictly to her home, between her and her husband and to seek for amicable solutions from within whenever the occasion demands. Where issues seem impossible to settle at home, it is better to seek the intervention of professional marriage counsellors than to run to parents who invariably may show bias for their own against the other.

2. The Principle of Cleaving: The act of cleaving involves being united, joined, glued, bonded, or blended together with one's spouse. It is not an event that happens at a particular point in a particular day. Cleaving is a process of growth, a daily process, of holding on and advancing against the forces that seek to divide or separate the couple. It ensures that a marriage endures hard times and still lasts! Properly understood, cleaving means that spouses are joined or essentially "bound" to each other for life with no room for dividing, depriving or separating (see Rom. 7:2-3 and 1 Cor. 7:39). Why? The simple answer is that cleaving is key in building a marriage that will endure hard times and be the beautiful relationship that God intends it to be. The Almighty God has emphatically stated that He hates divorce (Mal. 2:16) and that what He has joined together, let no man put asunder! (Matt. 19:6). The Lord advises every man to guard his spirit so as not to break faith with the wife of his youth (Mal. 2:15).

It has become fashionable these days for a man and a woman who are not married to live together in a sexual relationship and still call themselves a couple. In the advanced countries of Europe and the Americas where such arrangements are very common, they are referred to as "cohabitation." Invariable, there is no proper leaving such as by a customary marriage or a wedding and so there cannot be any proper cleaving under such arrangements. In Africa, such arrangements are frowned upon and those who indulge in them often pay dearly for their indiscretions. For example, a few years ago in Madina, a suburb of Accra, a disappointed family marched on a home and forcibly took away a woman who they claimed was their daughter. That woman had lived with a man for over ten years with children without any dowry ever paid by the man. Several attempts by the family to get the man do what was right and necessary had proved futile. While we do not approve of the extreme measures taken by the family to right the wrong perpetrated, the point being made is that the family neither accepted nor recognized the co-habitation irrespective of the long period involved. In an extreme case where the woman involved in a long-standing co-habitation died, the aggrieved family insisted that the offending man performed all the customary rites (which he had neglected for years) before the family agreed to co-operate with him in the burial arrangements.

The emphasis on the principle of "leaving" does not imply that one should go into a co-habitation arrangement without doing the right thing first. True and proper cleaving to one's spouse ensures that a marriage will endure hard times and go through the storms of life bravely and successfully. Proper cleaving ensures that marriages last because it draws on the love and commitment of both spouses for each other. Without cleaving, there cannot be lasting unity or satisfying intimacy.

3. The Principle of Becoming One Flesh: This refers to the physical aspect of the union between the husband and wife. It is just as important as the legal (wedding) and personal (cleaving) aspects. It is the will of God for every marriage to enjoy the true "one flesh" experience. This is a mystery. *"And they shall become one flesh,"* as quoted in Genesis 2:24 (NKJV), is a profound statement which means more than just the physical union. It implies that the couple shares everything they have, not only their bodies or material possessions, but also their feelings, hopes, aspirations, joy, fears, failures, disappointments and sufferings! In other words, the couple becomes completely one in body, soul and spirit and yet they still remain two distinct individuals. This is what really makes marriage a mystery. Any couple that cannot get to the point where they share all things freely, without holding back, without keeping secrets, cannot truly *"become one flesh."*

It is unfortunate that many people enter into marriage from the "union" or "sex" angle without first leaving followed by cleaving. The common trend is that the women in such situations usually get pregnant and the men are forced to marry them. Many of the men caught *in* such a web agree to the marriage as a compromise but not with their free will. The result is that many of these men have no commitment right from the beginning of the marriage and the relationship is bound to fail since they feel caged. Again, those who enter into marriage through the 'sex angle' usually miss the blessings of their parents because parental consent was either grudgingly given or was totally absent. The couple will find it difficult to properly "leave" and much less "cleave." Every marriage needs parental consent and blessings to really succeed and it is important this code is not overlooked or trampled upon.

Personal Secrets for Securing the Relationship

"Now, let me share with you my personal secrets that have helped my husband and I in securing and sustaining our marriage over the years. Don't make the mistake of thinking that we have never had our share of problems and challenges in marriage. Certainly, no marriage is immune to challenges. Every marriage faces challenges of diverse nature but how the couple reacts to the challenges will make or mar the marriage. Therefore, it is important that partners prepare their minds towards facing and overcoming the unforeseen but inevitable challenges," Mrs. Peterson added with a sigh.

"By the second year of our marriage, we felt that we had had our fair share of marital challenges. Hardly a week passed without one challenge or the other cropping up. If it was not about money, it would surely be about food, sex, in-laws or parenting. We needed to do something about the recurring frictions and conflicts. One fine evening, we sat together and thought through strategies to protect the marriage," Mrs. Peterson explained. "We realized that if we were to have a happy, lasting marriage, we needed to protect the marriage. We looked at the word "PROTECT." We brainstormed and turned it into an acronym to stand for the strategic decisions and approaches we needed to embrace in order to make a success of our marriage. We chose the words prayerfully since we believed they were to form the warp and weft of the fabric of our marriage. They are our secret gems that have proven to be more than precious stones of our successes. We have never openly shared with anyone, not even with our children, because we encouraged them to make personal discovery of their own success building blocks. But I feel obliged to take you into confidence with the belief that they will help you overcome your current challenges and ensure the success of your marriage. I have every confidence that things will turn around for good and that will be my greatest joy."

"My husband and I will take time to explain each of these building blocks in the acronym to you in our next meeting," Mrs. Peterson assured her and brought the session to an end with the firm belief that she had sown the seed of success in Nancy (and, by extension, also in you, the reader) with the help of the Holy Spirit.

Conclusion

Having come this far in her discussions with Mrs. Peterson, Nancy was completely overwhelmed but grateful for seeking the older woman for her counsel. She thanked Mrs. Peterson and promised to apply all that she had learnt from her and requested humbly that Mrs. Peterson considers her as one of her daughters. Mrs. Peterson happily accepted and prayed for Nancy out of her heart and blessed her.

It is encouraging that a lot of Christian couples go through some pre-marital counselling before they tie the knot. But the content and emphasis in these counselling sessions differ from Church to Church. It is our prayer that if you have read the counsel of Mrs. Peterson, you will apply your heart to these gems and resolve to make changes, first in your own life, and secondly, in your attitude towards your spouse and the marriage as a whole. That is the only way to protect the marriage so that it will flourish and last like that of Mrs. Peterson and surpass hers, "till death" do you part.

CHAPTER FIVE

BEING THE "PERFECT PARTNER" OF YOUR DREAMS

It usually begins as a fantasy while we are young and develops into a dream. We wish we will have the "perfect partner" when we grow up and marry. We begin to build stereotypes and develop a sketch of the "one and only" spouse we will want to spend our life with and to die for, if possible. Some of these fantasies get so ingrained in the sub-conscious mind that we tend to turn away possible suitors and keep hoping for "Mr. Right" or "Miss Right" to show up. Unfortunately, for some, the fantasy only turns into a burst bubble and an illusion since Mister or Miss Right never turns up.

Ben and Nancy Graham, the couple we introduced to you in the previous chapter had gone through such a battle of wits and self-righteousness. While Ben considered himself the perfect, Christian husband, he had always seen Nancy as the imperfect, problematic wife. On the contrary, Nancy believed she was the perfect wife and that Ben was the difficult one. And this kind of self-adulation has been the bane of many marriages and the underlying factor that triggers marital conflicts. When Adam passed the blame for their disobedience to Eve in the Garden of Eden, he was saying, "I am the perfect, obedient one and that Eve is the wild, evil one." From that day, it appears, many men have been blaming their wives for every conflict or misunderstanding in their marriage. But that attitude and posture must change in order to re-ignite the flame of love and passion between couples.

Six weeks after their last encounter, Mrs. Peterson ran into Nancy and her husband at the local supermarket. Nancy was bubbling with life but had forgotten to call Mrs. Peterson to give her a feedback. After exchanging pleasantries, Nancy with a broad smile said:

"Mummy, please, meet Ben my dear husband. Darling, this is Mrs. Peterson, my counsellor who has become a mother to me."

"I am pleased to meet you. I have heard a lot about you. And thanks for giving me a new wife in the person of Nancy," Ben quickly remarked while shaking the old lady's hand tenderly and flashing a steamy glance at Nancy.

Mrs. Peterson was beside herself with joy for meeting the couple in such a happy, romantic mood and she responded:

"You are welcome, my son. I am equally glad to meet you. You are blessed to have such a wonderful wife. Nancy is not only beautiful but she is also humble and intelligent. You two make a perfect match."

Nancy giggled over Mrs. Peterson's compliments and she thanked the old lady profusely before they respectfully requested to take their leave. Mrs. Peterson heartily agreed but reminded Nancy of their unfinished business.

UNRAVELING THE SECRETS

A week after the chance meeting at the supermarket, Nancy made time to visit Mrs. Peterson. On this occasion, Mr. Peterson who was at home and expecting Nancy joined his wife to warmly welcome her.

"Nancy, you are privileged to meet my King, Mr. Peterson, today. He decided to wait on you today since he has been following our pep talks and has been deeply enthused by your progress so far," Mrs. Peterson commented when they had settled down in the sofas of the living room.

Nancy politely acknowledged Mr. Peterson and thanked God for his and the family's life of marital, professional and spiritual successes. She was particularly awe-struck to hear Mrs. Peterson address her husband lovingly as "my King." She also took notice of the fact that the elderly couple sat together in the same sofa to welcome her home. These are new revelations to her since it is alien between her and her husband whom she calls by the first name, Ben.

Mr. Peterson retired recently as the human resources director of a reputable financial institution in the city. He is well respected in the financial circles as well as the Church. A distinguished speaker on human resources and management issues, Mr. Peterson brought his professional expertise to bear on the upbringing of his children and on his marriage in particular. Having experienced the drudgery of marital conflicts in the early years of their marriage, Mr. Peterson dug into his professional competences and prayerfully came up with the novelty of establishing strategies that will help protect the marriage. This did not come on a silver platter. It was after a heated argument one morning. The couple parted company and went to their individual offices. When they came home that evening Mr. Peterson, who had had a very bad day at work, was determined to find a lasting solution to the incessant skirmishes at home. He took the initiative and called his wife for a heart-to-heart dialogue. The outcome was their resolve to curtail their hurtful disagreements and to protect their marriage by charting a new course. Hence, the word *"protect"* suddenly assumed some special importance to them and they played word games with it until they turned it into a powerful acronym. Each of the letters in the word "protect" stood for a strategy that was needed if they were to protect and enrich their marriage. These strategies which they shared with Nancy are still evergreen and effective for any unhappy, hurting couples today who wish to turn things around for good.

Mr. Peterson explained that "the acronym, *PROTECT*, stands for: praying together, rekindling romance, overlooking wrongs, timeliness, encouraging each other, communicating effectively and togetherness."

At this point, Nancy took a notebook and a pen and began to write. She politely requested that Mr. Peterson repeated the words that constitute the acronym. Mr. Peterson did and added that he was ready to explain each of those constituent parts of the acronym. Let us join the Petersons and Nancy in that special session.

i.   **Prayer:** This is the primary duty and responsibility of every Christian and, for that matter, Christian couples. It is expected of every child of God to be prayerful and prayer should be seen as a special privilege granted by God the Father *through* which we communicate with Him. We thank Him for all His blessings and praise Him for who

He is. Indeed, prayer opens locked doors to the child of God and there will be no problem or challenge too difficult for God to solve when we go to Him in prayer. The Lord Jesus emphasized that *"if two of you agree on earth concerning anything that they ask, it will be done for them by My Father in heaven"* (Matt. 18:19, NKJV). The best example of two agreeing persons is a husband and wife. This is the key to marital success. It is a common adage that *"the family that prays together stays together"*. When a couple discovers this key and apply it in their lives, they live victorious lives irrespective of the storms of life that may buffet them. They will always be on top of issues and will not be tossed to and fro by them. When one is able to kneel before God, the one is able to stand before men because God will be there to lift that one up. This secret the Petersons, like many other successful couples, learnt the hard way.

According to Mrs. Peterson, when they discovered that prayer must be paramount in their marital lives, they embraced it wholeheartedly and set up a family altar. "We decided that we will no longer pray individually but will pray and read the Bible as a couple. We set apart special days for fasting for the two of us in the early days and later with the children. We also involved the children in our morning devotions which became a compulsory part of our family routines. There is no breakfast until we have had our morning devotion. The usual refrain is "NBNB" which means that "no Bible, no breakfast." Mrs. Peterson recollected that one of her favourite choruses on prayer was, and still is:

> *Prayer is the key, prayer is the key;*
> *Prayer is the master key.*
> *Jesus started with prayer and ended with prayer;*
> *Prayer is the master key." (Author unknown)*

Mrs. Peterson sang the chorus gleefully and was joined in by her husband and Nancy as well. After the singing, Mrs. Peterson continued and gave specific pieces of advice to Nancy:

"My daughter, make every effort to ensure that prayer becomes part and parcel of your personal life. Give yourself to prayer and see it as part of your food each day. Pray specially for your husband and his work. Ask for God's protection, provision and promotion for him always. Cover him with your prayer on his travels and against all forms of harm, danger and temptation. Pray likewise for the children and for the success of your marriage. A woman of prayer is a great asset to her husband. When you have time to pray, there will be no time for nagging and quarrels. There will always be peace and joy at home."

ii. Romance: It is sad that several couples gradually drift from being their romantic selves with the passage of time. The fire and fervour in a marital relationship are dependent on how the partners see each other as being romantic. As the marriage ages over the years, some partners become bored and take things for granted. Why? Simply, the fire of romance becomes almost extinguished. But the good news is that there are still embers that can be rekindled! Whom do you dress for and what does your dressing say about yourself? You must dress to please God and your spouse! Crumpled dresses, unkempt hair, body odour and poor communication are examples of things and behaviours that kill romance. Do you still feel the fire in your bones when you are in the company of your spouse? Are you leading separate lives unmindful of the feelings of the other? Those are sure signs that you are drifting apart and heading for the rocks. The romantic fire needs to be rekindled to give a spark of new life to the marriage. This must be consciously done and on a daily basis just as it was in the beginning.

Romance in marriage goes beyond bedroom issues. It involves being attractive and desirable to behold and to have. As a wife, how often do you visit the salon, change your wardrobe, the beddings and the curtains? After spending time and effort to prepare meals, how do you serve your husband? In the same old bowls and plates with chipped edges and on the same table with stained table-cloth? That poor attitude must certainly change. Change the serving dishes, the table cloth and napkins. Sit by him while he eats and pour him water if he needs it. That is one sure way of pepping up the level of romance in the marriage.

As a husband, when was the last time you appreciated your wife, her dressing, hairstyle and cooking? How often do you say "I love you" to her? Or is it only when in the bedroom? Do you find it extremely hard to say "I am sorry" until it is bedroom time? Do you have the habit of bathing and freshening up in the evening before bedtime? These and many more are things that spice up romantic love. If there is anything that women are never satiated with or are never tired of hearing, it is the simple words *"I love you"* from a truly loving and grateful heart.

An age-long enemy of romance is routine or monotony. Variety is the soul of a romantic life. So break the monotony. Put some spark into your way of life to bring romance back to flames. Endeavour to out-do each other in doing good by giving gifts and appreciating your spouse. This means that you put the happiness of your spouse above yours. Find him or her a nice romantic name and, better still, a name that is reserved or used only on special occasions and that has a story to tell.

"Ordinarily, I call him "Danny" and he calls me "Cindy," Mrs. Peterson explained. We also often call each other "Honey." But whenever I call him "my King" or say, "Will my King be going to the palace tonight?" the meaning is not lost on him. He perfectly understands that I need him. "On the other hand, if he should ask, "Will the Queen be attending the banquet tonight?" Or, "Will the Queen be ready for the party today?" I know and perfectly understand what he is communicating with me," Mrs. Peterson added.

iii. Overlook Wrongs: In every relationship, there is bound to be times when one partner would feel wronged by the other. But this is to be expected in an imperfect world with imperfect human beings. We offend others and also feel offended by others some of the time because no one is perfect. However, the most important issue is *how we react to wrongs and offences* rather than the real wrongs and offences done to us. It is a sign of maturity not to over-react but to be calm and overlook the wrongs of the beloved. Surprisingly, this is the case during courtship and the early years of marriage. The young in love are very much ready to overlook the wrongs of their partners. But, the same people find it difficult to let go when they are married and have been together for a while. The imperfections in them seem to loom large and the parties begin to notice the shortcomings in each other. Do you find yourself entangled in keeping scores? Then, you must remind yourself that true love *"keeps no record of wrongs"* (1 Cor. 13:5). Never make the mistake of referring to, or reminding your partner of, past wrongs and shortcomings. What is forgiven must be forgiven and forgotten, never to be brought back in the future.

It is said that life is not a bed of roses. Even if it were, remember that roses have thorns which may prick the one who picks them. In other words, one cannot get things going smoothly in life all the time. For this reason, the Scriptures have a lot of admonition for the followers of Christ. In Ephesians 4:26-27, the Apostle Paul advises that we should not allow *"the sun [to] go down while [we] are still angry [so that we] do not give the devil a foothold"* in our relationships. The words we speak may hurt our partners which may lead to anger. Anger, when not controlled and contained, may lead to other more hurting words, physical abuse, injury or even death. And the consequences are enormous!

How then can one ensure that the sun does not go down on one's anger? The Scriptures have lots of admonition on this for every child of God. The first step is forgiveness. The Scriptures enjoin us to *"forgive one another"* if anyone has a complaint or grudge against another (Eph. 4:32 and Col. 3:13). The second step is to *"love one another deeply"* (1 Pet. 1:22). Of course, *"love covers a multitude of sins"* (Pro. 10:12; 17:9; Jam. 5:20 and 1 Pet. 4:8). The phrase "a multitude of sins" is also translated as "all wrongs" or "all offences." This means that where there is love, disagreement and disaffection cannot thrive. They will be strangers. And this is true because, as the Scriptures say, *"there is no fear in love"* (1 Jn. 4:18). True or perfect love drives away fear and the 'lovers' or partners can enjoy a happy life. We have what it takes to ensure that we overlook the wrongs and offences of others since we also offend others.

The third step is that the partners (and the men in particular), must exercise great restraint when angry. We must show maturity by our self-control because any man who lacks self-control is compared to a city without walls or *"a city whose walls are broken through"* (Pro. 25:28). Any enemy can attack it since it literally has no defence. Little things easily irritate them and very often push them over the tipping point. In other words, lack of self-control makes one easily prone to anger and violence and many later regret their over-reactions in such moments of anger. Some partners, in their uncontrolled anger, have caused irreparable damages to their spouses for which they carry the guilt throughout the rest of their lives. Do you have a quick temper? Are you easily agitated or feel offended? Ask the Lord to grant you the grace to have self-control and to learn to truly forgive so that you can also be forgiven (Luk. 6:37).

"Let me tell you my personal experience with this issue," Mrs. Peterson said to Nancy as she beckoned to her. "A few days before our second wedding anniversary, I got angry with my King because I thought he was being insensitive to my condition. I was heavily pregnant and needed his help but he told me he was going out to keep an appointment. He promised to take care of my request when he returned. He then left me alone in the house and I felt ignored, abandoned and unloved. All kinds of thoughts raced through my mind when I heard his car being driven away. I even questioned myself why I agreed to marry him. I was down in spirit and boiling with anger for the unfair treatment I was receiving. Oh, how my man had changed!

"Two hours later, he came home and I did not respond when he greeted. I was still beside myself and wanted him to know how unloved I felt. He patiently listened to me while I rattled on and told him how uncaring he was. I was so upset that I failed to notice the nice gift bag he was holding. His response took me by surprise because there was no hint of anger in it but love and respect for me. He said softly, unlike in previous, similar marital battles:

"Darling, I am sorry to have made you feel awful. I went out for your sake. Happy birthday, my Queen."

He then presented to me a neatly done parcel with my name on it. It was there and then I remembered that it was my birthday. In my anger and confusion, I had forgotten my own birthday. Now, it was my turn to say, "Honey. I am deeply sorry. Please, forgive me." He stretched out his hands and we embraced. I have since then never forgotten the experience which taught me to overlook the wrongs, sometimes presumed, of my King."

Mr. Peterson looked at his wife with a broad smile across his face while Nancy nodded her approval. Nancy confessed that the incident was very much like one of her own running battles at home.

iv. Timeliness: If there is one commodity God gave in equal measure to all mankind, whether white or black, rich or poor, male or female, it is time. We all have the same number of hours in a day. But some are more able to make better use of their time than others. It is said that "time is money" yet many people do not see the truth in that adage. They forget that *"there is a time for everything ... under the heavens"* (Eccl. 3:1). Such people fail to factor time into their schedules to the extent that they lose the essence of timeliness.

Timeliness involves the ability to accomplish tasks within a specified time period or with enough time to spare. There is no room for procrastination. It also requires that things are well organized. What must be done ought to be done well and on time. A person who is time-conscious never gets things done late nor attends to issues and functions late. The Scripture describes the virtuous, excellent or perfect woman as having the habit of getting up at dawn, *while it is still night,* to prepare food for her household (Pro. 31:15). She makes sure that food for the family is never served late. The husband of the excellent woman never eats cold or late meals. No household chore is postponed or put on hold when time permits it to be done. How conscious are you of time?

When it is time to attend Church service or any programme for that matter, the time-conscious couple is always there on time. Would it be right to say that most men who attend to programmes late do so because of their wives? Unorganised wives are a big disadvantage to their husbands since they fail in their duties as home managers. To a large extent, this may not be farther from the truth. As a wife, how long does it take you to polish up for an outing? Are you able to get ready on time or do you have to complete polishing up in the car because your husband is in a hurry to keep an appointment? Does he have to blow the horn of the car to signal you that he is ready and waiting for you? Irrespective of the tall list of household chores or other responsibilities that need to be accomplished, if you are time-conscious, you will start in good time in order to complete on time for, say, an evening out with your partner. Every man is happy with the woman who is always ready to keep an appointment and on time. A man easily becomes jittery and stressful when he has to wait for a long time for his wife to get ready for a scheduled outing or appointment. As a wife, you will do well to spare your husband this ordeal.

"My mother-in-law was a wonderful woman when it comes to timeliness. She taught me to be time-conscious and get things done on time. If she had to travel, she would start packing up about a week to the time. She was always ready and waiting about an hour to every appointment she ever had. As a Women's Leader in the Church, she always made sure she got to the Church at least thirty minutes before any Church service began. Procrastination was not part of her vocabulary. It was certainly not in her veins. She executed all her duties almost with military precision. She was a well-organised woman. May God keep in perfect peace Auntie Dora (as she was affectionately called by all) for teaching and imbibing in me this valuable character trait," Mrs. Peterson testified and prayed.

"There is a time for everything, and a season for every activity under the heavens," the Scriptures confirm in Ecclesiastes 3:1. This is a wise saying and its import should not be lost on anyone: the preacher, business person, parent, athlete, teacher, student, soldier, politician, husband, wife and indeed every individual. Time lost or wasted is never regained so make good use of the time that you have now, when you can still accomplish your goals in life. The irony of all these is that we admire people who are time-conscious but we, ourselves, fail to be one!

Quite often, we allow several issues to clog our sense of time and we end up failing miserably to be timely in our activities. Such issues are known in the human behavioural literature as *"time robbers."* They are things and issues that subtly rob us of our time and cause our inability to keep to timelines at home or the workplace. They include procrastination, poor personal planning and scheduling, interruptions by people who do not have prior appointments but walk in and demand attention, poor delegation of work or assignments to the children at home or subordinates at the workplace, and poor use of the telephone as seen in spending unnecessarily long hours on the phone with one caller or client. It does not matter who the caller or client is. Telephone conversations should be kept short and precise since some other important calls may be waiting to reach you. Other time robbers are reading of junk mails, news or reports, poor use of the television, lack of clear priorities, indecision, and the inability to say 'No' resulting in over-commitment on the part of one or both partners. It is important for each partner to recognize his or her own time robbers in order to reduce their prowling on the most useful resource for every life, which is time.

v. Encouragement: We all need encouragement in one way or the other to make it to the next level in life. The Scriptures emphasize the need to *encourage one another* (1 Thes. 5:11; Heb. 3:13; 10:24-25). Couples must endeavour to encourage each other towards love and good deeds. This is the winning attitude for every couple. Encourage, edify and help your spouse to become that special person you so admire and want him or her to be. *"Two are better than one ... if they fall, one will lift up his companion"* (Eccl. 4:9-10, NKJV). A very typical example of two persons being better than one is the husband and wife. Where partners consciously and regularly encourage each other, they grow stronger and their marriage becomes better. A Bible teacher once remarked that "if you grow more spiritual and leave your spouse behind, that spouse will eventually bring you down." This implies that we must encourage our partners to climb up with us if we do not want to witness a downfall.

We all need someone to lean on at certain points in time when we are down in spirit, when the storms of life seem to overwhelm us. And if that someone is an encourager, he or she is able to lift up our spirits by the words of encouragement from him or her. This is where wives have the upper hand. They are natural encouragers since God made them "helpers" to the men. A few encouraging words from an excellent woman gets the husband back on track as if nothing has happened at all. On the other hand, a partner will lose faith and control when the spouse scolds and nags instead of giving words of encouragement. Words like: "Sweetheart, take it easy; it is well" or "Don't give up: the Lord is in control" or "We shall surely overcome," have the tendency to build up shattered dreams and restore the confidence of a downcast spouse.

For the common good of the partners, it is important for each to be a helper and an encourager like Barnabas! His name means the *Son of Encouragement* (Acts 4:36). When no one would want to deal with Paul after his conversion, it was Barnabas who led Paul and introduced him to the Apostles in Jerusalem (Acts 9:27). Eventually he became Paul's companion during his first missionary journey (Acts 13:2) and helped Paul a great deal.

Mrs. Peterson excused her husband and narrated how her husband encouraged her to go for further education. Turning to Nancy, she said: "At first, I did not see the need for such an educational venture. Our children were all in school and so I had enough time for myself. But I was thinking of how my King would fare when I should leave him for the university. How was he going to cook, wash, and keep the house since we had no house-help? I was worried that he was going to be 'home alone.' But he still encouraged me. I reluctantly agreed, but today, I look back and say 'I am most grateful' to my King. It was indeed a big sacrifice."

"I was a student for three years and my King consistently called me every day, sent me text messages and e-mails. I never felt lonely even though there were days I felt I was wrong in taking up further studies. He visited me on campus regularly and assisted me greatly with my assignments and research work by getting me the right materials and books. His words of encouragement made the pressure of higher education at my age very easy for me to cope with. If I am also a graduate today, I owe it to the support and encouragement of my King."

"The graduation day came and I was on cloud nine!

My King, the children, other family members and well-wishers were all around to share in my success and joy. I graduated among the top students in my class. It was a very special day for me. And that was not all. My King honoured me with a grand graduation party at which many dignitaries including ministers of the church as well as church members were in attendance. A very memorable day I will never forget, and all because I was encouraged by my King."

Mrs. Peterson then reached the bookshelf nearby and brought an album to show her graduation pictures to Nancy. Nancy took the album, flipped the first few pages and gasped, "I must admit, I am deeply humbled!"

vi. Communication: Communication is the heart-beat of a living, happy marriage. When a couple enjoys each other's company, they can talk for hours on end. This is especially true of any young couple who have just begun the journey into marriage. We can all testify to that fact. But as the years pile on, the hours spent together begin to shrink into minutes, and painfully, communication reduces to occasional "yes" and "no" answers for some couples.

The first sign of trouble in any relationship including marriage is the drying out or complete lack of communication. The power to turn your marriage around for the better is to keep on communicating! Keep on talking to each other. In the language of today's technological world, we will say *be on-line* and *stay connected!*

In order to achieve that objective, it is important that we explain a few things about communication. First of all, communication is a habit, a way of life, by which we share our thoughts and feelings. We share our ideas, dreams, visions, decisions and emotions as we communicate with the one we love or, generally, with our listeners.

Communication is a two-way affair. It always involves at least two persons: the speaker and the listener or the writer and the reader. In other words, there is always a *sender* and a *receiver* who must give a *feedback* to ensure that the message is well understood. Communication is incomplete without the receiver's feedback. Hence, it is always better to have one person speak while the other or others listen. When one spouse is speaking, the other must pay attention and listen. That is the bottom-line for good and effective communication.

The Scriptures enjoin Christians (and couples for that matter) to always *"speak the truth in love"* (Eph. 4:15). That is a mark of trust, love and confidence. How often do you speak the truth with your spouse? And how often do you spice your speech with love? Apostle Paul advised the Colossian Christians to *"let your speech always be with grace, seasoned with salt…"* (Col. 4:6, NKJV). Oh, if all married people will speak to their spouses in this way, how beautiful and enjoyable marriages will be!

In today's technological world, there are several gadgets and applications that enhance communication generally and between spouses in particular. The smartphone has revolutionalised communication. It was not so a few years back. During our growing years, we depended on face-to-face communication, letter-writing and telegraphic communication. Important messages were sent by special messengers who had to travel long distances to deliver them. A few years ago, when one needed to speak to a relation in a foreign country, say the United Kingdom, one had to book the call at the post office and wait for a day or two before the connection can be made. All that is history now. With our mobile phones, we can talk as much as we want. Couples can stay connected by using platforms such as Facebook, Twitter, Instagram, WhatsApp, Skype, e-mails and text messages, just to mention a few. Distance cannot be an excuse anymore!

An important principle underlying good and effective communication among spouses is to be sensitive to the feelings of your spouse and watch your non-verbal communication (Eph. 4:19). Actions, they say, speak louder than words. Facial and body expressions speak volumes, so watch them. Put away unwholesome talk, bad or abusive language. Stop reading between the lines and giving assumed meanings to the words your spouse speak! When you do not understand something, ask for clarification in a quiet, loving way. For goodness sake, put away bad temper, shouting, banging of tables, and tears. They do not solve any problems. Rather, they aggravate the issue and deepen the gulf between the spouses.

Be aware that communication can dry out in a relationship! When a couple is finding it increasingly difficult to have a happy, hearty conversation with smiles and laughter, it is a sign that communication is drying out. The good news is that no matter the level of dryness, communication can be revived by adopting a new way of speaking. Change your attitude or manner of speaking. Precede your speech with words like: "Please," "Darling," "Honey," or any other romantic name of your choice to catch attention. Or you can say: "Can I have a few minutes of your time, dear?" Such preambles are sure to open the door of attention from your spouse. So keep on talking. Keep the communication lines open. Remember that your spouse has no one else to talk to if you shut the door to communication. Such cold attitude or "silent trade" invariably pushes your spouse to seek a listening ear outside the home. You surely would want to avoid that at all cost.

Of course, it is important to give praise where it is due and to stress the positive in our spouses. Stop highlighting the negative side of your spouse! It leads to more hurt feelings and engender poor communication. For example:

> Don't say: "I know it. My spouse will *never* change."
> Say: "I know it. My spouse will *surely* change."
> Don't say: "He can't do this or that…," "It's impossible!"
> Say: "He can do this…," "It is possible!"

Acknowledge that you could also be at fault in any situation and admit your share of the blame. After all, "it takes two to tango." An American poet and writer, Ogden Nash, had this to say:

> *"If you want your marriage to sizzle with love in the loving cup, Whenever you are at fault, admit it; Whenever you are right, shut up!"*

In other words, a spouse should shut up when he or

she is right. Why? The attitude of drumming home the popular refrain, "I told you so," only makes the other party feel belittled, defeated or humiliated. The normal response is for the "humiliated" spouse to harden up and resolve to be assertive so as to score a point the next time. Avoid the "I told you so" syndrome so that the confidence of your spouse will not be dampened when you are right and your partner is wrong in a given situation.

Finally, every couple must learn to use a common language that they both can understand. It may be written, verbal or signs which can be sung or acted. It may even be a special perfume, clothing, colour, or food! A wink of the eye, a clearing of the throat, a snapping of the fingers, a slight tilting or nodding of the head, and a soft whistle are some of the strategies a couple may use to communicate between themselves and unknown to the people around.

Above all else, it pays good dividends to adopt the use of the golden expressions: "I am sorry," "I love you," "I am proud of you," "You are a darling," and "I am grateful you married me." You can be sure that no woman is ever tired of hearing these expressions, especially "I love you," for the umpteenth time in a day! As men, let us do well never to allow this expression dry out of our daily communication with our spouses. We were good at saying it in the early days before marriage. Why are we now running short of it? Let us rekindle the romantic fire and see it burning brighter the more we say "I love you" to the Only One!

"My dear Nancy, I wish to say with emphasis that you should take care not to treat communication with your husband as a trite issue," Mrs. Peterson came in. She continued: "Give it all the attention it deserves and speak to him with deep respect because he is the head of the family. As a matter of importance, know when to talk and when not to bother him with long conversations. You know that women love to talk and when the timing is right the conversation becomes even more interesting. When your husband arrives from the office or a trip, do not meet him with a long list of problems you have encountered while he was away. Give him a warm welcome, with a hug and/or a kiss. Give him good food to eat and sit by him while he eats. In fact, it is even more romantic to eat together. When he is more relaxed and composed, he will be ready to hear you out.

"Discuss issues from the point of view of humility and respect. Give him the opportunity to have the last say and allow him to make the bigger decisions. Ensure that you do not openly disagree with him and never contradict him in public, before the children, friends, associates, church members or the general public. From time to time, ask him what food he would like to eat and do well to prepare those meals for him. It does not have to be any special day or occasion. I hope that these tit-bits will go a long way to ignite a fresh spark in your marriage," Mrs. Peterson concluded. Nancy expressed her understanding with gratitude.

vii. Togetherness: "I am excited to talk about the last of our strategies which have underpinned the success of our marriage," Mr. Peterson remarked. "Togetherness is the lifeline to the success of all human relationships. In marriage, togetherness is an outward expression of how secure the partners are. Unfortunately, it is the missing link in several marriages today. No wonder divorce and separations are on the ascendancy among the married and, in all cases, the children end up being the biggest losers.

Why do some couples find it difficult to be together or to be seen together? It should be easy to be together. However, in Africa, some people are afraid of getting too close to their spouses because of some old customs and suspicions which have become barriers. For example, where a husband is seen to be too close to the wife, there is the presumption by the man's family and friends that the wife has cast a spell on the man. So, for the fear of this suspicion, some spouses find it difficult to be seen or to be doing things together. Where there is anger or an unresolved conflict between the couple, some spouses refuse to shake hands or respond to greetings. But these negative attitudes do not help anyone. They rather draw the couple wider apart and must be curtailed forthwith.

From the first family, Adam and Eve, we learn that God's intention was that the couple should be together all the time. Jesus confirmed this truth when he said that the man and his wife *"are no longer two but one flesh"* (Matthew 19:6). Some Bible scholars believe that as long as Eve kept the company of Adam, the devil could not get at her. The devil succeeded in deceiving Eve when she was found alone. Where was Adam? Had he been with his wife at that material moment, mankind may not be groping under sin today! Granted that the opinion of the Bible scholars may not be correct, the need for couples to be together cannot be underestimated. Even if it is not possible for a couple to be together all the time, they should seize every opportunity to be together. That is the best and only way to build oneness into the relationship.

When you were courting, you cherished being in each other's company. In the early days after marriage, you were proud to be seen together. Do you still cherish the company of your spouse or you feel you should lead your separate lives now? Be careful not to open the door for the devil to attack your marriage by keeping a distance between you and your spouse. Close the gap and treasure being together.

Every married couple should endeavour to spend quality time together, just the husband and wife. Have time for hearty conversations with smiles and laughter. Laughter is good for everyone; it is a mark of both psychological and emotional health. Consider the fact that healthy babies are those who laugh a lot. King Solomon revealed to us in Proverbs 17:22 that, *"A cheerful heart is good medicine, but a crushed spirit dries up the bones."* So, couples should go ahead and pray together, worship together, study the Word of God, eat, bath, visit, travel, sleep, walk, and laugh together, among many things. Togetherness is very important because it leads to *oneness*, which is the hallmark of a happy, lasting marital relationship.

A very important aspect of togetherness is touching. This involves the physical care and attention we give to each other. Physical contact, apart from sex, is essential for keeping the flame of romantic love alive. Couples should find it easy to hug or embrace each other, hold hands, sit close together, squeeze the hands, and kiss without being ashamed. It is a good practice for a couple to sleep together in the same room and on the same matrimonial bed! It is also biblical. When two people lie down together, they keep warm (Eccl 4:11). How can one keep warm alone in his or her own room? Besides, research has shown that babies and children get accustomed to their mothers first and well because of the constant touch they have between them and the mothers. Touching builds a solid bond between the persons involved and couples who are good at touching benefit greatly from the practice. If you have not been doing it, begin it today and watch the transformation in your relationship.

"Truly, being together has been one of the secret strands of our success story," Mrs. Peterson happily remarked. "We decided very early in our marriage to be together no matter the odds. Although we did not know or call it togetherness then, we were happy to be in each other's company. We did several things together besides praying together and having our quiet times or morning devotions. We fasted together, cooked and ate together, washed our dirty clothing at the weekends together. My King was always on hand to assist me and to be by my side. It was rather a difficult task bathing together the first time. But we found it to be fun. Have you ever tried bathing together with your spouse, Nancy?"

Nancy shook her head and said, "No." She said it would be difficult for her to do so and wondered whether Ben would welcome it. Mrs. Peterson encouraged her saying, "Don't force him. You may start in a simple way by asking him to bring you the towel which you left behind or call him to give you a good sponging at your back. He will not deny you this invitation and make sure he enters the bathroom. He will admire you even if he says nothing. On another day, while in the bathroom, you may invite him to join you in bathing together. If it should lead to intimacy, give in. After all, the objective is to bond you together. We have done it several times in the past and I enjoyed it all."

"A bigger boost to our togetherness has been my accompanying my King on several of his numerous travels, both locally and abroad. By the very nature of my King's job, he had to travel a lot. As much as possible, I made time to accompany him. His colleagues and friends grew accustomed to seeing us together such that some also began to travel with their wives and no longer their girlfriends or mistresses. Do not turn down any opportunity to accompany your spouse, even if it is just visitation to family members, friends and colleagues at the workplace or church members. The major advantages of being seen together are that it protects your spouse against temptations towards infidelity and enhances the chemistry between you as a couple. The more people see you together, the more they admire you. You may carve a special identity for yourselves by wearing the same fabric with your spouse to important functions including church services. Grab every opportunity to make people around you know that you are one with your spouse and that you are 'the special one.' My last words to you will be the evergreen advice Queen Elizabeth gave to her daughter: *"You may have been born a princess, but you must learn how to behave as a lady."* In other words, you must make special efforts to apply all these pieces of advice and strategies in order to reap the benefits as a married woman."

Conclusion: Nancy was beside herself with gratitude to the Petersons for the time spent with her and the pieces of advice given her. She said that if this had been one of the usual marriage seminars, she would not have had enough money to pay to attend. Or, even if she did, she would not have benefitted from the pieces of experiential advice from Mrs. Peterson. "Mum, you have made me feel like a woman again and I believe that Ben and I will be forever grateful to you. I have gone through a school and I promise to apply all that you both have taught me. God richly bless you!"

The Petersons prayed with Nancy and asked for God's intervention in renewing her marriage for the better. Nancy then said goodbye and took her leave.

CHAPTER SIX

YOU CAN MAKE THE DIFFERENCE

It is never too late to do anything one desire's to do in life. It is all a matter of attitude, commitment and determination. Walt Disney, founder of Disney World Theme Parks, is credited with the saying that *"if you can dream it, you can do it."* If you desire or dream to make your marriage work, you can do it. It depends on you, but not on your partner. Be the change agent and it will motivate the other too to change. You cannot change your spouse. No. The change you desire must begin with you and the ripple effect cannot be lost on your spouse.

Steve and Maggie Darko had been married for over two decades now with two teenage children. To their families, close friends and associates, it is a miracle that the Darkos are still together as a couple. This is because their challenges as a couple began from day one at their wedding reception and it became 'normal' to hear them quarrel and fight openly and aggressively over the years.

Things got out of hand at the plush wedding reception when, in giving wine to his bride, Steve's shaky hands spilled the drink into the expensive, immaculate white wedding dress of Maggie. Maggie could not control her emotions and spewed venom on her husband which confounded most of the guests. Some respected elderly persons including their parents helped quell the looming inferno that threatened the very foundation of the marriage from that day. Thereafter, it had been quarrels and fights galore. Hardly a week passed without the couple having one misunderstanding or the other. Perhaps, what contributed to their being together for that long were Steve's frequent travels as a sales executive of the company he worked for. Nonetheless, any time the couple was at home, there was bound to be some arguments and hot exchanges since they had lost the joy of having any effective communication between them. On a few occasions, they had threatened to divorce but Steve had always backed out of it since he believed he was the cause of it all from day one.

Years ago, in one of Steve's travels up country, he was invited by a friend to attend a marriage seminar at his church. Steve was reluctant but yielded to his friend's persistent reminders. That seminar became the turning point for Steve. He saw it afterwards as God's answer to his numerous petitions and prayers.

"I attended the seminar as a mark of respect for my friend," Steve began his testimony.

"I went early to the church but took a back seat. Being a marriage seminar, lots of people came in as couples. I felt a bit uneasy because I was alone. My friend came with his wife and invited me to sit with them in the front seat. I politely declined. The service was very lively and unlike any other I had attended as far as I could remember. The praises, the dancing and the spirited prayers of the congregants were all new to me. When the time came for the speaker to take the microphone, the auditorium became silent. Everybody seemed expectant and they were not disappointed. The speaker did justice to the subject matter on communication between husband and wife. Most of his examples were reflective of my own situation as if he had had a fore knowledge of my predicament. But I knew that was not the case. I took it all in good faith and felt it was God who led me to the seminar. I asked God in prayer to help me apply the things I had heard in my own marriage. A few of the things I took from the speaker that day were: *'you cannot change your spouse; you can only change yourself;' 'what you expect from others, do it for them first;' 'you can make the difference'* and that *'real love is sacrificial: it always asks, "What can I do to make you happy today?"'*"

"After the service, I went to my friend to thank him profusely. He was happy that I came and hoped that anytime I visited their city, I will find it worthwhile to fellowship with them. I gave him a firm promise. That night, I could not sleep. I thought about how pleasant the couples who attended the seminar looked. Why was mine different? What can I do to change things for the better for Maggie and myself? I cried to God for strength to apply the things I learnt from the seminar. But I was afraid of how Maggie would take it all.

"I arrived home from my trip to meet Maggie who, as usual, barely acknowledged my presence. The cold reception was not new to me so I did not complain. When we went to bed that night we slept at the edges of our big bed as usual with about three feet of space between us. Nothing had changed. But I was determined to bring changes into our marriage. Early the next morning, before Maggie could get out of bed, I rolled over to her side, supported my head in my palm and on my elbow, and said: "My Love, what can I do to make you happy today?"

"My words seemed to have jolted her as she abruptly sat up on the bed, stared at me with scorn and asked, "What did you just say? Did I hear you well?"

I slowly repeated my words: "My Love, what can I do to make you happy today?"

"Oh, I see. You can go clean the bathroom if you care," she retorted with scorn and left the bedroom.

She was apparently expecting me to meet her fire for fire as we used to do. But I gathered courage and stayed calm. Cleaning the bathroom was a chore I had never done and Maggie never thought I would do it.

"In the next one hour, I cleaned the washrooms and the toilet bowl, polished the tiles and the sink, removed the silt from the choked drains and the window panes and made the washrooms look entirely new. I was happy with the result of my labour. There was no compliment from Maggie at all.

"The next morning, I asked Maggie the same question: "What can I do to make you happy today?" Again, in the same uncaring, lackadaisical mood, she yelled: "Go trim the hedges and plant new flowers."

That was quite a heavy task but I was ready for the challenge since I had some days off from work after my long trip. I did that job to the best of my ability and it gave the house a new look. I was happy with the work I had done even when Maggie pretended not to have seen anything.

For the succeeding two days I kept asking Maggie the same question until either she grew tired of giving new assignments or felt embarrassed by my requests. For me, it was fun doing something that benefitted my family and which, I hoped, would make Maggie happy. And it did. This is because on the fifth day when I asked the same question, Maggie's response was, "No. You can't do anything."

"Yes, I can do anything," I replied.

"Why are you doing this to me?" she asked with teary eyes.

"Because I love you, Maggie. I care about you and our marriage," I answered and quickly added, "Forget the past. We can open a new chapter for our marriage. I have made a commitment to spend the rest of my life in making you happy."

"Me? Why me? I thought it was over between us," Maggie asked amidst sobs.

"Not at all! I still love you, Maggie," I said that while reaching out to hold her hands. She willingly allowed me to hold her hands for the first time in several months. I drew her closer and said, "My Love, what can I do to make you happy today?"

"You will have to tell me what happened during you trip. You are a very different man now. I am sorry I have given you so much pain and unhappiness in the past years. But now, 'What do you want me to do to make you happy?'"

"Not so fast. I asked the question first. I promise to tell you what happened during my trip up country."

Maggie could not give any new assignment. She left for her office in a sober mood with the expectation of coming back to learn about the secret of Steve's transformation since his return from the trip up country. Steve took the liberty to arrange her perfumes, hair sprays, lotions and other accessories on her dressing table. He decided to surprise her with a dinner prepared by himself by the time she returned from work. Incidentally, Maggie came home a lot more early that day from work. Though not her usual buoyant self, but there was a tint of change in her gait and demeanour. As Steve anticipated, she was taken aback when she went into the kitchen to prepare dinner and found it already done. Steve went further to tell her to sit down so he could serve her. The couple ate their dinner together on the same table for the first time in several years! It marked a real turning point.

That evening, Steve had a lively chat with Maggie without any fight. He told her about the marriage seminar he attended and his resolve to make amends to save his marriage. For the first time, both shed tears together for hurting each other with their words. Maggie for the first time in more than a decade knelt before Steve and apologized for her uncouth behaviour at the wedding reception. She said, "I feel ashamed looking back. I don't deserve your love for the pain and disgrace I brought to you. I have been difficult to live with as a wife. I am the problem and not you. Please, forgive me."

For the next few weeks, Steve continued to ask the question "What can I do to make you happy today?" The couple took it to be fun asking to do things that would make the other person happy on daily basis. While Steve stuck to his question, Maggie varied her own by asking questions like: "What would you like me prepare for dinner tonight? Which of your shirts would you like me to iron for you? Which suit or tie would you like me to make ready for you? Which of your shoes would you like me to polish for you?" Steve and Maggie now try hard to outdo each other in making the other happy. Indeed, true love is sacrificial. Are you there yet? Surely, you can make the difference!

LOOKING BACK

According to a renowned marriage counsellor, Tom Mullen, *"happy marriages begin when we marry the ones we love, and they blossom when we love the ones we marry."* Steve and Maggie, the couple we met in the previous section, must have learnt that lesson the hard way. Many of us may not be able to stand the disgrace Steve faced on his wedding day. But, it has been said that "it is not over until it is over." Loving the ones we marry has been a challenge over the years across the globe. But it is achievable. We tend to grow in love where there is commitment and mutual respect for each other.

A happy, successful relationship or marriage does not just happen. It must be worked upon. It is an art that must be learnt. A brand new car requires regular maintenance and care to keep it functioning perfectly. So it is with any human relationship including marriage. Marriage is also likened to a garden that requires skilful, constant and delicate tending in order to have the desired results. The beauty and splendour of a loving relationship depends on how much effort the partners are prepared to put in. Anything short of that will see the marriage soon overgrown with 'weeds' that eventually will choke it to death.

Several beautiful, fairy-like marriages have hit the rocks because the partners never got committed to working for the success of their marriage enterprise. Once a partner looks over the fence and sees the greener grass on the other side, it is very easy to fall into the deadly trap of thinking that it is rosy over there. What most people forget in such frenzy moments is that someone must have been dutifully watering the grass on that side. If they would realize that they could equally achieve the same greener grass by faithfully and lovingly watering their own lawn, many relationships would flourish better and last longer than what we are seeing today. Are you being tempted to think that yours is doomed for failure? Are you not realising your neglect of watering your own lawn? It is not too late to do something positive about your situation. You may be asking, "But how can it be done knowing that things have gone out of hand for far too long?" Take a deep breath and move on to the next section.

LOOKING FORWARD

The task of mending broken fences is not an easy one. It is better to take good care of the relationship so that it neither develops cracks nor suffer breakages. Some of the practical ways of keeping the fence intact and the grass greener are outlined below. They are not in any special sequence but those who have prayerfully followed them have witnessed outstanding transformations. It is our prayer that yours will be no exception as you dedicate yourself to apply these truths.

i. Renewed dedication and commitment to our Lord Jesus Christ: This is in recognition of the preeminence of Christ in the life of every Christian. He is the witness of the marriage covenant and He will grant the grace and strength to overcome the challenges. It is important that the couple considers this issue together and invite the Lord Jesus Christ to take His rightful place in the relationship. Very often, couples who are facing challenges are found to have either put Christ out of the relationship or have pushed Him far away. Their personal relationship with Christ is often at the lowest ebb, if not completely shattered. There is, therefore, the urgent need to restore the relationship with Christ.

ii. Renewed love and commitment to your spouse: Having settled it with Christ, the next thing to do is to settle it with your spouse. It requires renewing your love to your spouse and showing commitment to him or her. This amounts to providing his or her needs lovingly without compulsion. Seek the happiness of your spouse and you will equally be happy.

iii. Mend holes in your relationship and stay focused: This is the time to say more of "I love you" and mean it. Begin to pay your spouse compliments such as: "You look more beautiful or handsome than I first met you," "You look gorgeous in that dress," "I like your hairstyle, it is beautiful." Commend your spouse for a good meal, a great evening, or a wonderful time of conversation. Show appreciation for little things done and done well.

iv. Make a definite decision to stop chasing the mythical greener grass. This means making conscious efforts to water your own lawn and ensuring that it stays greener over time. Concentrate on the positive and desirable qualities of your spouse while purposely playing down the negatives, if any. As a husband, it is your responsibility to make your wife look good, if not better, than the other woman.

v. Open a fresh page in relating to your spouse from today. Start doing again for your spouse some of the things you used to do for him or her when you first met and married. In addition to paying your spouse compliments, you must begin to lend a helping hand in the chores around the house. There are a few basic things you can do to help your spouse. Wives do appreciate husbands who can fix basic electrical or plumbing problems without calling in a technician. You can lend a hand in cooking, washing, ironing, trimming the hedges, or mowing the lawns. Someone has said that, "When a man learns to fix the "front office" problems, the "back office" issues are taken care of naturally."

vi. Forgive and tolerate each other: There is nothing in a relationship as sweet as being completely forgiven by a loved one whom one had offended. It is a natural as well as a spiritual way of healing wounded hearts. Whatever had caused the pains in the past are wiped off and a clean bill of health is accorded the other party. While our inability to forgive and tolerate each other has serious implications for the survival of the relationship, harbouring grudges and keeping malice have negative health consequences for our very selves. When spouses fail to talk to each other on account of a misunderstanding between them, they tend to miss a heartbeat whenever they meet around the house. Such irregular heartbeats and feelings of being scared on seeing the partner is a recipe for high blood pressure and other cardiac conditions. Make room for the shortcomings of your spouse. Raise your tolerance level for your spouse's inconsistencies and errors. After all, you also make mistakes and offend others as long as you remain human but not an angel.

vii. Seek appropriate help as and when necessary: It is a good decision to seek help early for any challenge the couple encounters which are beyond them. There are several common relationship issues that when left unchecked could lead to serious challenges with dire consequences. They include delayed pregnancy, miscarriages, frequent misunderstandings, family planning, medical problems, in-law issues, finances, and lack of respect for one another. Regular medical check-ups, counselling from matured Christian leaders, psychologists, financial and investment experts, among others, are pertinent in keeping the health of the marital relationship. Of course, any resort to external assistance must be with the mutual consent of both parties to avoid unnecessary suspicion and mistrust.

MAKING THE DIFFERENCE

Ever since the days of Adam, and throughout mankind's history, the married had always experienced an unfathomable joy before, during and for a few months or years after the wedding. Adam's exclamation on waking up and seeing beautiful Eve by his side that she was the *"bone of my bones and flesh of my flesh; she shall be called 'woman,' for she was taken out of man,"* (Genesis 2:23) amply demonstrated his excitement. Since then, nearly every man has felt the same excitement, at least on the wedding day. And it has always been the unwritten prayer of every married man that his wife will permanently stay as the same beautiful, understanding and caring woman that he married. What most men overlook is that they must also remain the same handsome, strong and romantic man that the woman married. Therefore, before expecting a change in your spouse, show the way by changing yourself. When you lead by example, it becomes easier for the followers (here, your spouse and children) to imitate you. A Chinese proverb says that, "Riches adorn the dwelling; but virtue adorns the person." This means that you can have an outward display of your wealth in the kind of dwelling place you have. But character cannot be displayed that way; it is innate, in-born and defines who you are. The virtues you cherish to see in your spouse must be seen in you first.

One fine afternoon, Mr. Peterson came home to be informed by his wife that they have been invited to a dinner by the Grahams. Ben and Nancy wanted to express their gratitude to the Petersons for helping them put their marriage back on a sound footing. An elaborate dinner had been planned with a few invited guests including their Pastor, family and friends. The guests of honour were no doubt the Petersons.

The Petersons had arrived to a very warm welcome by the Grahams whose youngest daughter, Angie, presented a beautiful bouquet of fresh spring flowers to Mrs. Peterson. The old lady remarked that it was reminiscent of her wedding reception many years ago. Since most of the guests had already arrived and were seated, the Grahams wasted no time in starting the function. The Pastor prayed as usual. The food and drinks that were served were good. The music was cool and the whole atmosphere was heavenly. The evening turned out to be an occasion for the Grahams to outdoor their new-found love.

After the dinner, Mr. Graham took the stage to tell their story and it became clear that the Grahams were a different couple now. Their animosities had whittled away and have now been replaced with love and laughter; a very happy family indeed! He was full of praise for the Petersons whom he described as *"the architects of our new marital life."* He added that "the keen interest the Petersons took in us, the invaluable pieces of advice given us and their prayerful support when the going was tough have brought us this far."

"We have learnt the hard way that success in marriage is more than *finding* the right partner. It is *being* the right partner," Mr. Graham emphasized. He also postulated excitedly that "Your spouse is your best reward on earth. Therefore, you should show deep appreciation and affection to him or her. There is nothing wrong with your spouse if you accept that God gave him or her to you. The greatest mistake we make is to find fault with the spouse while indulging in the belief that we are perfect. The fault is the other party's, not mine. I am a saint and he or she is the villain. I had held the same views until we met the Petersons. They had the patience to school us in the principles underlying happy marriages and the strategies every couple needs to know and apply in order to break through and be successful. Nancy and I will forever remain grateful to the Petersons who have now become our parents."

The Grahams brought out a beautifully wrapped package and invited the Petersons to receive it. When the package was opened, it revealed an intricately crafted chandelier which received a loud applause from the guests. The splendour of the gift left everyone awestruck. As to its value, no one was left in doubt that it could cost a fortune! A fitting present to a special couple who gave everything to ensure the transformation of a marriage that was about to hit the rocks. Nancy, while making the presentation said that the value of the joy and new-found love that have enriched their marriage cannot be quantified. The gift was a token to the Petersons to show their appreciation.

"Mummy, I want to state that when I took your advice that I should change myself and not try to change Ben, things started to work better. Like the proverbial phoenix rising from the ashes, our marriage has received a new vigour and momentum of life. And here we are today: changed, refreshed and bubbling with happiness as if we have just been married," Nancy said so emphatically.

She turned to Ben and gave him a passionate kiss. The guests could not help but give them a standing ovation.

The Petersons received the gift with great joy. But they were not to be outdone. They also came with a beautiful parcel of a marvellous, gold-plated wall clock which they presented to the Grahams. The most fascinating thing about the clock was that it had been programmed, on the hour, to chime the popular John Fawcett (1740-1817) hymn:

> *"Blest be the tie that binds,*
> *Our hearts in Christian love;*
> *The fellowship of kindred minds,*
> *Is like to that above."*

The clock was set in motion and guests who knew how to sing the hymn joined in the singing. Suddenly the atmosphere turned heavenly and when the function came to a close, everyone was satisfied that it had been a memorable evening indeed.

CHAPTER SEVEN

RISING FROM THE ASHES

The story of the Grahams is typical of many marriages today which are going through real challenges and are probably on the brink of collapse. The Grahams successfully turned their fortunes around by heeding to the pieces of sound biblical and experiential advice from the Petersons. They were able to rise from the ashes, as it were, to become a bubbling, loving family again. Surely, you could also benefit from the lessons they learnt from the seasoned Petersons which are shared in this book. The marital challenges you are going through are not beyond recovery. It is not too late to prayerfully give it a try. After all, what is impossible with man is very much possible with God (Matt. 19:26; Mar. 10:27). So, do not throw up your hands in the air and say that your marriage is beyond repair. God is on your side to help you if you will invite Him to do so.

The Darkos, on the other hand, presented a different facet of the dynamics of marital challenges. We hope that you did not condemn Steve for keeping his vows and holding on to Maggie in the face of the traumatic experience he passed through on his wedding day. It is refreshing to identify with the Darkos who equally rose from the ashes to become an example of marital success. Both the Grahams and the Darkos recognized the need to work on their marriages and to let go of the issues that threatened the survival of their marriages. Instead of allowing their conflicts to hold sway over them, they rather accepted their differences and were ready to celebrate them. That is a positive outlook which confirms the adage that "where there is a will, there is a way."

If you maintain the attitude that your marriage is beyond recovery, your partner will never change and that you have had enough, then nothing can be done to help you. You must change your attitude towards your spouse and your marriage. The difference between success and failure is *attitude*. Thomas Jefferson, as President of the United States of America, once said that, "Nothing can stop the man with the right mental attitude from achieving his future. Nothing on earth can help the man with the wrong attitude." As long as the marriage has not been dissolved, there is hope for rekindling the dying embers by fanning it into a bonfire of love. It all depends on your attitude towards your spouse and the issues that are threatening to tear you apart. You have what it takes to turn things around and to make your wife "the special one, the only one" again and for good.

In his commentary on God's blue-print for marital success as written in Genesis 2:18-24, Matthew Henry, the 19th century theologian, aptly stated that:

> *"The woman was made part of man, out of man, not from his head to lord it over him, not from his feet to be trampled on by him, and near his heart to be loved by him."*

In other words, God Almighty had good reasons to choose a rib from Adam's side to create Eve for him. She was to be loved by him and not to be treated shabbily or to be ordered about as if she were a slave or, worse still, a mere sex object. She was to be seen as being part of your bones and flesh. For that matter, what you would not do to your own body should not be done to her. What you love to do for yourself or expect to be done for you is what you must equally do for her. That is the right way to help her become the "special one, the only one" that she was created to be for you.

The process of turning things around for the better can be cumbersome and protracted. In recognition of the enormity of the challenges involved in making a fresh start and in rising from the ashes, the following are set down as guidelines to facilitate the transformation. It is our prayerful belief that having had the patience to come this far, you are willing to ask for God's assistance through the Holy Spirit to begin the reconciliation and transformation processes. The Lord will grant you good success. Here we go:

1. Even if your marriage is labeled as "Made in Heaven," it must be worked on here on earth to succeed. No one lives his or her marital life in a fairyland. No matter how good a piece of machinery is, it requires regular maintenance to work perfectly. Similarly, it does not matter how nice a garden or lawn is, if neglected, it will be overgrown with weeds. So is the marriage relationship: it must be worked upon regularly in order to keep it fresh and green. To "live happily ever after" does not come on a silver platter but requires a lot of hard work by both partners and the personal commitment of both to ensure success.

2. Don't try to change your partner; **change yourself!** You must be the change agent to engender the change you desire in your spouse. The experiences of the Darkos are typical of the need to begin a change revolution from oneself. When you change your attitude towards your spouse for good or bad, your spouse will respond in like manner. A good attitude engenders a good response and a bad one is met with equally a bad response. For instance, when you speak lovingly to your spouse, the response will be equally charitable. On the other hand, when you shout at your spouse, you should be sure to receive a shout in response. So, kick-start the change process by yourself and your spouse will follow suit.

3. Never reduce your spouse to a piece of property acquired for the home! Your spouse is part and parcel of yourself. You loved her, cherished her company and were generally proud of her before you tied the knot. Why do you now feel ashamed to show her off? You do not like her clothes? Change her wardrobe! Pay for her salon visits. Take her out to dinners, corporate get-togethers and on shopping. Take her along on your treks and trips as appropriate. Make her feel she is the queen of the silver realm you survey. And, indeed, she is the Queen!

4. Good communication is essential. Speak to her always in love with your speech seasoned with salt. No harsh words. No insults. No abuse. Be honourable to admit your mistakes (Prov. 12:22; 28:13) to make for easy resolution of conflicts or disagreements. Never insist on your right (1 Cor. 13:4); it only makes you hard to live with. Do not brood over little misunderstandings. Seek a quick resolution so that it does not degenerate into a marital war. Be bold to say "I am sorry" and mean it. Treat her with respect as the weaker partner and as heir with you of the gracious gift of life (1 Pet. 3:7).

5. *Find out and meet your spouse's needs from her viewpoint.* Seek her best interests and not yours. When she is happy, you will be happy too. Let your spouse feel he or she is the most important person (the King or Queen) in your life. You may lose your job, health, finances, friends, and even parents but your spouse will be there to give you succour. Treasure her because she is *"all you have ... under the sun,"* *(Eccl. 9:9)*. When the going gets tough, you can be sure that she will be there to offer you encouragement and a helping hand where possible.

6. *Spend quality time together.* Make the time to be with her, hold hands, pray, sit, eat, bath, laugh together. Isaac left us a wonderful example to follow (Gen. 26:8). Just the two of you (without interference from the children) makes a world of difference! Take a weekend out of town and be together either for a retreat or just another honeymoon. As much as possible, attend concerts, cinemas, weddings, funerals and other social events together. This will strengthen the tie that binds you together.

7. *Learn to give gifts to one another; make it a habit and not an occasional drop in the ocean!* It is a beautiful way of keeping the fire of romance burning brightly. Couples who strive to outdo each other in good deeds never feel bored or frustrated in the relationship. There is always a

surprise, something new, awaiting you and the very thought of it whips up the thrill of being together. Decide to give the most important person in your life a gift today and watch the warmth it will trigger.

8. Encourage and build up one another daily towards love and good deeds (Heb. 3:13, 10:24). Give her a shoulder to lean on. Help in her educational advancement. Encourage her to go for higher education and pay for it. Help her to explore and learn new things. For example, she may want to learn to play the guitar, organ, or the trumpet. Or she may want to learn how to play lawn tennis, golf or badminton. Give her the support and push her towards becoming a "better" person than you first met her. Endeavour to add value to her life. It is always a plus when both of you share the same interests and explore new ones together.

9. Show appreciation for little things done in love. A word of appreciation spoken at the appropriate time gives enough motivation for your spouse to do more and better. Pay her compliments on things she has done or can do very well. Compliments on things that she is naturally endowed with and which she cannot control do not amount to much in her estimation. For example, saying that she has beautiful eyes is a good compliment but will not be appreciated as much as if you had said that her choice of colours well matches the colour of her eyes. This is because having beautiful eyes is natural; she does not control that. She was born with them. But appreciating her colour choices or matching clothes tips the scales! Appreciate her family and friends. These are the persons who reinforce acceptance of your very person. Compliment her character and personality over her physical attributes. Above all, compliment her intelligence!

10. Bring variety and creativity into the marriage by doing things differently. According to William Cowper, an English poet (1731-1800), "variety is the very spice of life, that gives it all its flavour." Variety kills boredom and provides a new lease of life to the relationship. Therefore, remember to change the beddings, curtains, menu, and the position of the living room sofa and others from time to time. Dare to be different by changing your hairstyle, clothes, shoes, and your romantic life. In the words of the English philosopher, Francis Bacon (1561-1626), "nothing is pleasant that is not spiced with variety."

11. Take good care of your body by maintaining quality personal hygiene. This needs not be overemphasized. It is a basic requirement. Take regular baths and showers, twice everyday: one in the morning and again in the evening or at night before going to bed. The undergarments must be given a special care with regular washes. Trim the beard or be clean shaven and groom the hair well. Take good care of the mouth by brushing regularly and especially after meals. Avoid all kinds of body odour by using deodorants and sprays that do enhance the aura around those who wear them and add to their confidence. You should do well to smell good always!

12. Be committed to the success of the marriage. Nothing is more important than your personal commitment towards ensuring the success of the relationship. You loved each other and that is why you both agreed to tie the marital knot in the first place. Therefore, see every difficulty encountered along the way as a challenge that is resolvable and which should bind you together the more after a happy resolution. Where both parties are committed to each other, there is no challenge that will be insurmountable. You can both sing out loud: "Whatever my lot, Thou has taught me to say, 'It is well with my soul.'" God is right on your side to give you success because He is the Witness in your marriage (Mal. 2:14). And that gives the assurance that no matter the storms you may be passing through you can rise up again to celebrate your love.

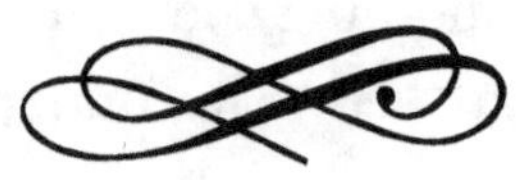